MASK

MASK

MY RACE THROUGH THE BELLY OF HOLLYWOOD TO SELF-DISCOVERY

ELI WEHBE

MASK

My Race Through the Belly of Hollywood to Self-Discovery

ISBN   978-1-5445-2617-1 *Hardcover*

        978-1-5445-2616-4 *Paperback*

        978-1-5445-2618-8 *Ebook*

        978-1-5445-2619-5 *Audiobook*

CONTENTS

AUTHOR'S NOTE

I have changed the names of most people in this book, out of respect for their privacy. All the events in this book are real and true, described here to the best of my ability to recall and describe them.

ONE

BIG FISH

"I think everybody should get rich and famous and do everything they ever dreamed of so they can see that it's not the answer."

—JIM CARREY

THE LAST DAY OF JANUARY 2018 WAS A TYPICALLY beautiful, chilly morning in Studio City. I bounded out of my house at 8:30 a.m. and jumped into a rental car. My Mercedes S 63 AMG was at the dealer's because the transmission was acting up. This white C-Class was a loaner. The leafy neighborhood was quiet except for some minor road construction.

I'd worked the night before, as usual, but had an ironclad routine: late nights, early mornings. I was on my way to the gym for a long run and then a sweat. Only ten days before I had completed my first half-marathon, in Pasadena. I was on a path to become a better person in every way, and my newfound commitment to running and fitness lay at the heart of that journey.

I made a right turn out of my driveway and noticed a half-dozen odd-looking cars in my mirror—undercover cop cars. That was odd. Then I heard the sirens and saw flashing lights in the mirror as they hauled ass to get right up behind me. I took another turn, and the cops waved me over.

What the hell is going on? This must be some kind of mistake.

Except I wasn't on the run.

"Roll down all your windows and put your hands on the steering wheel!"

The megaphone was loud and insistent. I rolled the windows down and put my hands on the wheel. At least, I thought, they'd pulled me over on a quiet street, where I was less likely to be embarrassed in front of my neighbors.

Two people dressed in casual clothing, apparently undercover officers or detectives, approached the car. One stood back while the second, a woman in her thirties, came up to my window as I rolled it down.

"Where are the keys to the front door of your house?"

What the fuck?

"Can I ask why I'm being pulled over?"

"We have a search warrant for your home and for certain items to be seized, one being your vehicle. Where is your car? Where's the S 63?"

Search warrant? What the hell for?

I should have asked to see the warrant, but the thought didn't even cross my mind. I'd never been arrested. I'd never faced a situation like this in my life. I'd never been pulled over except for a speeding ticket and window tint. I felt completely rattled.

"The keys are here, in the cupholder," I said, adding that my car was being serviced.

"Get out of the car," the cop said. She made me sit on the curb.

"Should we cuff him?" one cop asked another.

"Yeah, let's play it safe. Cuff him and let him sit in the front seat of your truck."

Another group of undercover agents took the house keys and walked back toward my home. I knew they were about to go through it from top to bottom.

Who were these guys? They were dressed in street clothes and driving nondescript cars. Were they Los Angeles police? Sheriff's deputies? State cops? I didn't know, and nobody was telling me.

I felt like a criminal, and I didn't know why.

As I sat in the truck, trying to make small talk with the officer next to me, some pieces began to fall together in my mind. In the back seat, I could see folders containing printouts from an LA gossip website that had been hounding me. I could see enough to know they had something to do with a thirty-year-old model named Amber, who had died from an apparent drug overdose a few months earlier. She was found dead at her friend's apartment more than five hours after leaving a party at my house.

Shit.

I was a partner in one of Los Angeles's hottest nightclubs, a big fish in the shark-infested swimming pool that is the hip, hot, sexy world of LA nightlife. And right now, half a dozen cops were fishing through my house, my rented car and my life, hoping to hook me.

TWO

THE VISION

"I like entrepreneurial people. I like people who take risks."
—BILLIE JEAN KING

THE DOWNTOWN HOLLYWOOD NIGHTCLUB THAT WAS my Mecca had everything.

There was a full-service Asian fusion restaurant with a carefully crafted menu, a basement with live entertainment and a dance floor, a third-level banquet and event center with food service, and a main-floor dancing and live entertainment space.

The best part was a spectacular, design-driven rooftop lounge. There you'd find cabanas, a bar and bottle service, and stunning 360-degree views of Los Angeles, including the legendary Hollywood sign.

This was Kress, a club right on Hollywood Boulevard.

One night in early 2009, my girlfriend Melissa and I approached Kress's doors for the first time with a friend who knew a promoter hosting an event on the roof. The team at the door whisked us past the line of people trying to get through the velvet ropes and straight upstairs.

I loved that feeling of *getting in*. It is the rarest of currencies in Los Angeles after dark, the thing everyone wants. It gave me a thrill.

On that perch above the city, I ordered a sugar-free Red Bull, gazed out at the Hollywood sign, and turned to Melissa with a huge smile.

"This is it!" I declared. "This is where I belong! I have to find a way to get in here and get hired. I can get my career in Hollywood nightlife started up right here, right now!" In that moment, I made myself a promise.

By the time you are twenty-eight years old, you are going to own your own nightclub, Eli.

As we chatted with other people on the roof, we soon came across the promoter working the event: Dilon. He looked like your typical promoter: deep V-neck shirt, chest out, flashy jewelry, a ton of gel in his hair. In other words, pretty scummy. Like someone you'd see on a cheesy reality show.

We spoke for a bit, and then I put my question to him.

"How did you get started promoting in Los Angeles?"

That was all he needed to start *selling* me. He told me that he was The Man, that he was living the Hollywood dream, that he accomplished this and that, that he knew this famous person and that celebrity—you get the idea.

Of course, I didn't believe a word.

Actually, I believed every word. I was the new kid, and I would find out pretty soon that I had a lot to learn. But that night I looked at the beautiful girls and seemingly cool guys standing with Dilon. I ate up how he seemed to fit right into this scene that I so desperately wanted to belong to. And I believed everything he told me.

I didn't yet know the game in this city.

I would come to understand that most of what he told me was absurd lies, misleading information, and made-up stories. That's what you get from 99 percent of people in the nightclub industry. They'll say anything, because the most important thing to them is to look cool in the moment, so they can gain clout and advantage in the conversation or the situation.

"Dilon, listen," I said, leaning in. "If you have any kind of connection to get me in to promote a night with you and your team here at Kress, I can 100 percent bring a weekly crowd of girls and guys that will meet the standards here. I've done it before, and I can do it again."

I didn't know it at the time, but I'd just set myself up as a mark.

Dilon looked me over. "If you think you can bring a hundred people and sell a table or two, I can pay you 1,200 dollars for the night. We can get started Friday."

I felt like a little kid at Christmas who had just received the video console I'd been begging my parents for.

"Done! See you next week!"

The next morning I raced back home to the dry, hot Moreno Valley. I lived there with my parents, who are the only people I've ever really looked up to in life. As far as I'm concerned, my dad, who emigrated from Lebanon to the United States in the 1980s with nothing, is a straight-up hero. He worked his ass off to provide for me, my sister Diana, and my mother. He was an electrical engineer—but also an avid marathoner. Tony is six-one, with a thick Arabic mustache, fluency in French, English and Arabic, and a short temper. He'd give you the shirt off his back, but he was a tough-love kind of parent. There was a lot of yelling when I was growing up.

The whole neighborhood was scared of him. If he drove up the street while I was playing basketball with other kids, they'd yell, "You're dad's here," and scatter. He'd get really mad if we were playing basketball in the front yard and the ball landed in his plants. He would yell at me in front of everybody, and his temper was scary. He'd yell about the stupidest things—once he chased me around the yard with pruners because of something I'd done. He'd get angry about the smallest things.

When I played basketball in eighth grade, he would yell at me to run faster. I was kind of heavy then, and although he didn't call me "fat," he was hard on me. I trace my lack of patience and my short temper to him.

We loved to make fun of Dad's accent. English was his weakest language, and he has a funny habit of adding "sss" to words where it doesn't belong. He'd say things like, "Son, let's run to Walmartsss." We all found this hysterical. He'd say, "Screw you guys," in his Arabic accent, and then we'd laugh even harder.

My mom was a homemaker who showered Diana and me with love. Food was her love language, and she filled us with Lebanese specialties like hummus, stuffed grape leaves, and mezze. She made it clear that, no matter what I did, no matter what happened, she loved me. When my dad was yelling at me, she was the one who saved my ass. She still calls or texts me every day, as she always has done. My parents don't drink, and my mom was very clear that she didn't approve of alcohol, drugs, or premarital sex. She taught me strict Catholic morals and made sure we all went to church every Sunday—even my dad, who had a long period of not believing in God but still went anyway.

Diana and my mom, Laure, were really close, both of them very religious. There are only two years between us, but Diana and I didn't see eye-to-eye on many things, and we went different directions in life. She stayed on that religious path. I was the rebel.

Even though I had a good home life, and I loved my parents, I was not proud of my heritage. Like a lot of first-generation Americans born to immigrant parents, I wanted to fit in. My neighborhood was mostly white and Asian, and I got picked on a lot as a kid, for being Arabic at a time when the U.S. was at war in the Middle East, for having thick eyebrows and parents with funny accents. I always felt judged, and I was ashamed of my culture. I hated when my parents spoke Arabic in public, and when my dad haggled with everyone for everything. The whole scene made me cringe.

I loved my family dearly, but I didn't want to stay in Moreno Valley any longer. The Inland Empire where our home was seemed a long way from the glitz and glamour of LA. Now I had my ticket out. Geographically, Moreno Valley was only seventy miles east, but culturally it was a world apart. It's the land of *bros and hoes* tattooed head to toe with lifted trucks, the 909ers, and bandana bandits. Yeah, I came from a small town, but I believed I could succeed in the big city. I knew I would make a name for myself.

As for the name...I went by Elias until a very cool, very beautiful friend named Hannah said to me in middle school, "You should use Eli. It's short, it's hip, it's cool. I like it!" Well, if Hannah—who was a middle school boy's vision of heaven on earth—liked it, that was good enough for me.

Eli? Deal!

I felt like the name made me cool. In fact, I was a serious computer nerd addicted to playing online games. My favorite was Counterstrike, a multi-person first-person-shooter scenario pitting terrorists against counter-terrorists. I was a gaming addict, involved with the best clubs and teams, playing for hours every day for days at a time. My butt literally went numb from all that ass-in-the-chair time.

I slurped down every kind of soda you can think of, snacked on Sour Patch Kids and Twix, and inhaled juicy Carl's Jr. Double Western burgers, all while playing at my console. You name the junk food, I ate it. I kept my eyes glued to the screen and headphones on, and spent my days yelling at my teammates into my microphone: "Copy that! I'm going in! Cover me!"

I felt and looked like the Pillsbury Doughboy. Gaming at the turn of the century wasn't the big deal it is today. If I'd known what it would become, I would have continued to master that world and remained chunky, unhealthy, and unaware. Luckily, I did have some awareness. I began to see myself for what I was: an overweight teenager with no drive or passion in life, becoming useless to the larger world, sitting around and eating like a pig all day.

If this isn't helping me grow physically, mentally or financially, I have to let this gaming addiction go.

And so I did. I quit cold turkey. I am very binary in my commitments—either all in or all out—and it was time for me to be out. I turned my attention to my future.

I was surrounded by skinny friends who ate whatever they wanted, drank whatever they wanted, and never gained a pound. They were the popular kids, and I craved their acceptance. I wanted to be the cool guy, so I bleached my hair to get the "slim shady" a.k.a.

Eminem rapper look, changed up my entire wardrobe to "skate-boarder cool" (baggy shorts, skate brand T-shirts, skate shoes) and began boarding around town, a chubby kid trying to fit in.

In eighth grade I started playing basketball religiously. It became my life and meant another full wardrobe change-up. I was determined to fit in with this new scene and new crowd.

All of this grasping was driven by my insecurities. Every few years something else swallowed me up as I chased one sparkling light and then another that I believed would lead me to happiness I didn't feel. I never lived for myself. Instead, I always lived for the acceptance and approval of others. And I never accepted myself for who I was.

I spent a lot of time at my friend Tyler's house up the street. His father was a firefighter, and the family had a beautiful home on a hill, with a pool and a view of the city. It seemed to me that his father, working in a career that served and helped other people, had built a beautiful life for himself. I wanted those things, too: a purposeful, meaningful life and nice possessions.

The good life.

That motivated me to get serious about putting my life in gear. I wanted my life to start, and now I wanted to become a firefighter. I hadn't enjoyed school up to that point, but by my senior year in high school, I was ready to move fast. I enrolled in an honors home-school program to speed up my final year so I could get on with learning how to be a firefighter. I didn't have any patience for traditional education, and I didn't see any value in actually learning something because I was told to learn it. If I didn't believe the coursework was going to be directly beneficial to me, I hacked the system.

In my younger years—and I'm not proud of this—I cheated my way through school, even though I'm a terrible liar. If I had been caught, I would not have been able to pretend or fight my way out of it. Anybody talking to me can tell in a heartbeat if I'm not telling the truth. Some people lie through their teeth on a daily basis, but you couldn't pay me to do it. I suck at it anyway!

One reason I cheated was that it was incredibly hard for me to learn in classrooms. I have Attention Deficit Disorder. Forty-five seconds into a lecture, my attention had wandered to someplace else.

What am I going to do for the rest of the day? What are my friends doing right now? What should I eat when I get out of this prison cell? Is this what I want to be doing? Why am I even here?

Where cheating didn't work was in Spanish class, which didn't interest me at all. You can't fake your way through a language you don't understand. It was the toughest class I took. I know now that in the real world, in real-life situations, you have to put in the hard work. You can't dodge the process or cheat the grind if you truly want to learn or advance. You get back what you put in—a life lesson I would have to learn the hard way. I didn't understand it back then.

My goal was to get through high school and into college and start making some money. The thing is, I had fallen in love, and that love demanded cash. The object of my desire was a Chevrolet Silverado Z71 pickup truck, off-road tuned with twin-tube shocks, electronic hill descent control, a two-speed transfer case, and an automatic locking differential.

It was a thing of beauty.

My dad offered to co-sign on a car loan so long as I attended college and held down a job that covered the car payments. Urgently, I began to search for jobs all over the city. I could smell that dream truck.

Eventually, a friend of a friend connected me to a construction company that hired me as an assistant to the superintendent. With that, my dad co-signed the loan, and I got the truck!

My boss was a tough-love guy. When I started work I was seventeen years old, 6' 2", 230 pounds. A lot of that was flab. My dad had been tough on me, but this was a whole other level. At the time I didn't understand why the boss was so tough on me, but now I see that he was truly strengthening my mind, body, and soul.

The company built tract homes in Moreno Valley. I did whatever my boss asked, grinding hard for five days a week doing heavy outdoor work, cleaning homes before inspections, or whatever else came up. The temperature could be a hundred degrees while I worked my ass off, sweating like crazy. My body had never experienced anything like that. The first week of work, I dropped ten pounds.

That inspired me; I liked the feeling of losing weight. I got a gym membership and became a full-on gym rat. I didn't miss a day, no matter how tired I was, no matter how tough work was. In three months I dropped sixty pounds. I became obsessed with looking thin, so much so that I became anorexic. Anorexia is characterized by a distorted body image and an unwarranted fear of being overweight; a typical anorexic tries to maintain a below-normal weight through starvation or too much exercise. That was exactly what I was doing.

I did two hard workouts a day and ate a single, massive meal of mostly protein. I was determined to keep cutting weight, even though my ribs were starting to show. My biggest fear was to be chubby again.

Finally, my mom called me on my insecurities. "Elias, you have a huge problem," she said. "Your father and I are seriously worried about you. We need to fix this, and fix this now."

Like most teenage boys, I didn't take well to being told what to do. As far as I was concerned, I didn't have a body image problem (another symptom of anorexia), and I wasn't insecure.

Why should I listen to my parents when they clearly don't know what they're talking about? I'm right and they're wrong.

I felt amazing on the outside, super skinny and thin. No reason to change my anorexic ways, my mind said. But my body began to rebel. I felt fatigued every day, sometimes flat-out exhausted. More important, my mind wasn't right. If I stood up suddenly I might black out, my vision blurry or vanishing for a moment. I was on the job every weekday, dehydrating myself in the heat. It wasn't a good situation.

As much as I hated to admit it, I could see my parents were right. Something was wrong with what I was doing. I began to change my eating habits, eating more, spacing my meals out to two or three a day while staying slim.

I told myself at the time that I had an "extreme personality"— that's why I went so all-in on things. That was a lie. The truth is, I had, and have, an addictive personality. Addictive behavior was my way of dealing with my insecurities. It has been the root of most of the problems I have faced. I have learned, the very hard way, that sooner or later I will have to face the truth about that personality. Like it or not, your truth will catch up with you in life, and if you are not ready, it will hit you smack in the face harder than you can imagine. That's when you discover where your true strength lies—how you're going to pull yourself out of your own hole and find the courage to create a different mindset, and a different path, for your present and your future.

I would get there, but it would be a long road.

* * *

When I was seventeen I fell in with an entirely new and pretty unsavory crew I called "the rough riders." They were older than me, rebels who lived on the edge, hanging out in grungy bars and tattoo shops and doing pretty much whatever they pleased. I went back down the acceptance hole, flipped my wardrobe again to baggy pants, grew a Mohawk, wore a bandana tied around my head, got snake-bite piercings on either side of my mouth, and got my first tattoo. (I already had the required jacked-up truck, at least.)

We spent a lot of late nights in dodgy bars and a night scene that involved plenty of fights. My crew was a bunch of obnoxious, heavy drinkers, although nobody that I knew was into heavy drugs. I didn't like the fighting—my way is to avoid conflict and work things out—and I didn't drink much, as I don't much enjoy alcohol. I stayed pretty sober because I figured somebody had to look out for these degenerates.

My strictly moral Catholic parents had no idea what I was doing, which was the opposite of what they wanted me to do. I didn't care—I was determined to develop my badass image and fit in with my new friends. Of course, that image was nowhere near who I actually was, and I came to see that I was going to have to get out of this gang—because it was a gang—before I really found myself in the wrong place at the wrong time.

I'm a firm believer in karma. If you do good, you will experience good, and if you do bad, well...bad shit was happening to these people and their families. I had to get out gracefully. They weren't going to break my knees or kill me if I left, but if I ghosted them they could make my life difficult. Strangely, my exit opportunity came in the form of the worst barfight we experienced. We all came out of it torn up, bruised, and bloodied. We definitely could have ended up behind bars. This was my ticket to freedom. Look,

I told them, this isn't for me. I have a different path to follow. They knew I had their back, and they were all cool. Occasionally I'd get a text or a message from someone in the gang checking up on me, but I was pointed in a different direction and didn't look back.

I had outgrown them. All of us outgrow people in our lives, as we come to realize they no longer serve us, that there is nothing more to be learned or gained from a relationship. Eventually, if we're lucky, we learn who we are, and learn to be true to ourselves. I was a college boy now, not a rebel badass, and I turned my attention to my freshman year at Riverside Community College.

Except my ADD was a major impediment. Classes were a snooze-fest. I had immense trouble focusing on what the teacher was saying. I dozed off in my squeaky chair at my tiny desk. I stuck with it for months, hoping for the fun part of learning to be a firefighter to begin. But it didn't.

Instead, when I finally got into a class to learn about becoming an Emergency Medical Technician (EMT), the instructor hit me with cold water. "This will be hours and hours of heavy and intense book work and text work," he said. "It will take up most of your days and nights. This is not for everybody—repeat, not for everybody. I suggest you call it quits if you aren't ready for this to be your entire life."

I respected that. After all, we were learning how to save lives. We needed to be fully committed to a very serious subject that needed focused attention. But...that was not for me. What he described was not what I could do; I knew that much about myself. I was back in school again, the kind of school I hated, and it was driving me nuts. I could see my dream of becoming a firefighter slipping away.

What am I going to do?

A few weeks before that EMT class began, I visited an old friend at his house. His dad gave us some advice. "Son," he said to my friend, "you have always been very quiet and shy. You have no choice but to go to school to succeed in life. Elias, the truth is, you have a good mouth on you. You definitely have a *loud* mouth, but it will pay off in the long run. You know how to talk to and deal with people. You have a gift—school or no school, you will figure it out. I believe it. I *know* it."

That stuck with me, and it sticks with me to this day. My mouth—my ability to talk, cajole, convince—was an asset. Maybe I could do something with that.

I began to think about something else, too. When I was in high school, a nightclub promoter who worked at a nearby Redlands nightclub called the Rock 'N' Saddle contacted me through my MySpace board, where I was pretty active. "You know a wide variety of people, Eli," he wrote. "I could put some extra money in your pocket if you could attract more people to come out on certain nights."

How hard could this be? I got to work. Using my MySpace bulletin board, I quickly showed I was able to get cool guys and edgy girls to come out to the Rock 'N' Saddle. It was my first taste of life as a nightclub promoter. I did that for a few months, polishing my social skills and my ability to sell people on the excitement of nightlife. The money was nice, but after a while, my attention drifted elsewhere, and I stopped promoting.

Now, as I watched my dreams of becoming a firefighter crumble in the face of daunting coursework, I began to think about working in nightlife again. My friend's dad's bold statement—"you have a gift—school or no school, you will figure it out"—popped into my mind as the EMT class teacher warned us about our need to commit. I knew then that school wasn't the path for me. I left that class, and college, and kept going.

I had something to prove. I was a kid from a small town, and I wanted the world to know I could do big things. I wanted to be accepted on an entirely new level (there's that desire to be accepted again), and the Hollywood life I had seen on television while growing up appealed to me. Every celebrity who was anybody in LA went to nightclubs, so why not work to become The Man of the nightlife world? I could network and connect with the right people and grow my brand, because I wanted to be a brand in my own right. And I could get what every young guy dreamed of: money, status, beautiful girls, a luxury home, expensive cars.

I would achieve the Hollywood Dream.

* * *

That was the story I had in my head the night Melissa and I went to Kress. After meeting Dilon, I was convinced I was on my way. I came home fired up and got to work right away, jumping onto my MySpace bulletin board. (Yeah, it was a while ago!) I announced that I was working now at Kress nightclub—and let me tell you, that did it! I rallied my friends and friends of friends. I was promising them something new—a night out in the Hollywood nightlife scene that they couldn't get otherwise—and they wanted it. As a promoter, I promised them that they would get into the club quickly and smoothly, that they would have fun, that if they needed a table I would set them up.

This is beneficial to both parties. Them and me. You're going to make a career out of creating a social space to host your friends with great entertainment, Eli!

I was pumped. I quickly sold two tables. Each buyer would be required to spend a minimum of $1,100 on bottle service. I had a hundred names on my personal guest list. (I later learned that most promoters, people who have put years into the grind, have trouble selling a single table a night and getting fifteen or twenty people to come out consistently.) Established promoters get a cut of whatever their clients spend—usually 10 percent, but more, even 20 percent, if the promoter is really good. Clearly, I was going to earn the money Dilon promised me.

My list was mostly girls and just a few guys.

After all, rules are rules.

If you were a man on my list, you were there because you were a close friend of a woman on the list and were bringing more girls, or you purchased a table and were going to be spending a lot of money at the bar.

Here's the brutal truth: Men come to a club and spend.

Their value to the club is *money. Moolah. Bread. Dough. Cash in the till.*

They do that because the club is full of hot girls. And why are the girls there? Girls come to clubs because they want to meet attractive and successful men. Men who will spend money on them.

You may like it or not like it, but that's human nature, and clubs are set up to facilitate it and take advantage of it.

The formula was simple, and it became a mantra I repeated to myself many times in the years to come: *Girls, girls, girls! The money will flow and the rest will follow.*

The exception was celebrities. If you're a celebrity of some sort, you get a free ticket right through the velvet ropes and that strictly guarded door. Promoters, club owners, and the door team all have the same goal: to curate the best, most attractive crowd who will spend the most money. Their approach is part formula (girls!) and part art. Who's the hot celebrity this month? Is that bald hedge fund manager nobody knows going to drop a ton of money? Is this B-list star starting to get noticed in the trades? Does this guy know the owners? Everything revolved around status and outside appearances.

Generally, if you don't meet those requirements—beautiful woman, rich guy, or celebrity—or have some sort of relationship with the owners or a promoter, *fuhgeddaboutit*. You're not getting in.

Friday came at last. Game night! I left home early, around 8:30 p.m., and drove the hour-and-a-half to Hollywood. I was nervous, excited, and ready to host. As I drove into the city, I blasted house music, windows down, cruising through downtown LA to my dream destination: Hollywood.

Let's do this, Eli!

I arrived early at Kress. Floor lights were shining into the sky, as if they were summoning me. *Na na na na na na na na na na na na na, Batman!* I felt like I was in the movies.

List in hand, I was ready to get this night booming. I approached the red ropes in front of the back entrance. Celebrities tended to use the more discrete back entrance, which led from a parking lot to both the rooftop and the basement. The front entrance went to the restaurant and the second floor.

"Hey, guys," I said to the staff I found there. "I'm Eli. I'll be working with Dilon and the promotions team. Where should I go for the time being?"

Nobody acknowledged me. At last, a woman in a long coat and black leather boots, who was drinking a cup of coffee, got up off her chair and strolled over to me. She had short blonde hair, a silver hoop lip piercing, and killer green eyes.

"Nice to meet you, Eli," she said. "No one told us anything about you, and I'm not sure I know a 'Dilon,' either. Let's just wait for the rest of the team to show up. Hang outside for now."

Huh? Okay...

I spent the next few minutes talking to the door team and other employees. None of them had any clue who I was or what I was doing there. Nor did they care. At all. They seemed to have no idea that I was working that night.

Soon the head door guy pulled up—Jared. He was calling the shots, and it was clear that he had full control over that door. You always need a guy like Jared at a legit nightclub, someone to *keep it right, keep it tight*. He was tall, fit, suave, with long brown hair and a terrible attitude. He was a full-on asshole. People either really loved him or really hated him. It was his job to be that way, because he was the curator-in-chief. He decides who's good looking enough, who looks like a big spender, and who is trying to slide in on some promoter's list but doesn't make the cut.

I tried to introduce myself to him.

"Hey, Jared, my name's...umm...umm...Eli. I'm...uhh...working with the promotions team tonight." I could hardly get my own name out, I was so nervous.

He barely looked at me, nodded ever so slightly, and walked away. Straight-up ghosted my ass.

I was getting a very fast education in how the nightclub business worked. Nothing was going to be simple. I was going to have to earn my stripes.

It didn't help that while all this was happening—or *not* happening—I couldn't reach Dilon. He wouldn't reply to my texts. I was really starting to stress out.

Wow, is this really happening before the night has even started?

I took a breath.

Stay calm. Stay positive. Buckle up. It's going to be a rough night, Eli.

Finally, Dilon arrived. He definitely was not being cool. He had his head down and looked like he didn't want to talk to me. "Sorry for not replying to you," he said. "I was dealing with a situation."

Whatever that meant.

But okay, he was here. Everything should run smoothly now.

The doors were about to open. The door team was setting up, making sure it was *right and tight*. Showtime!

Except—I could see nobody on the team liked or cared about Dilon. "Go back inside, Dilon!" Jared yelled repeatedly. This was the guy who told me he was The Man? I saw a very different reality from where I stood inside the doors, nervous and insecure.

Like I said, I was getting a very fast education. Dilon was full of shit. That's usually how it goes in Hollywood. People play the part they need to get what they want. They nail the script and become great actors. Of course, it's Hollywood! What else should I have expected? You can't trust a damn word anyone says. It's Phony Island.

I was confused, uncomfortable, discouraged, and embarrassed. I could feel the sweat on my face. And that was *before* Jared's team started turning my guests away at the door. My friends and friends of friends! Holy fuck, this was becoming a disaster.

What should I do? Call it quits? Admit to these people that after all the hype I had pushed out, I couldn't get them in?

I'm not a quitter. I adapt. I figure shit out. I most definitely was not going to be embarrassed in front of all these people I'd invited to Kress. Once I've said I'm going to do something, I will do it. I will not give up until it's done. I had told these people they were going to get into Kress, so I had to get them in somehow.

I've got to figure this out. I've got to finesse this situation.

Two older Latino guys in T-shirts and khakis were off to the side, talking regularly to the girl running the list. It didn't take long to figure out that they were making the calls about who got in and who didn't. They seemed to be in charge. (I would come to learn that in Hollywood the richest, most powerful people were often the ones who didn't seem to worry about what they wore.)

I had to get my people through the door. Their door.

I had no friends here. No one was going to rescue me. I had to figure this out on my own.

"Yo, my name is Eli," I said to them when I saw an opportunity. "I know you guys don't know me, but I'm working with Dilon—"

"Oh, he's a sub-promoter," one of them said. He was Roger. His partner was Jake.

"Long story short, he told me he ran this, and he would pay me."

"All right, what do you need?"

"I just need to get my people in. I already sold two tables for 1,100 bucks each."

Once I told them that, they agreed to help me out.

I had a terrible time that night. I stank of stress-sweat. In the coming months and years, as I got deeper into the world of nightclubs, I learned that my personal stress on a given night was usually balanced by positive feedback from the guests I had helped, hosted, or welcomed. The worse my night was, the better theirs was. That's just the way it goes in this game.

As the night wound down, I found Roger on the dance floor and explained what Dilon had promised me.

"That weasel Dilon is lying to you," he said. "He's a sub-promoter for another promoter who works for Jake and me. He probably took all your hard work and just put it under his name, so he looks like an all-star to the promoter he works with. I'll let my team know what happened. Come by Tuesday, and you can explain the entire situation."

I couldn't reach Dilon. Didn't see him, couldn't find him, and he wouldn't answer his text messages. It dawned on me that this wasn't his first rodeo. But I also knew it wasn't going to be my last. I had learned a lot that evening. He had sized me up, scammed me fast, and taught me a lesson about this beautiful, dark, twisted business.

The following Tuesday I was back in LA, explaining everything to Roger and Jake at a café where they were paying out their promoters.

"He told you how much? Twelve hundred dollars?" Roger sounded incredulous. He shook his head. "He really did scam you. I'm sorry, but we don't even have you on our payroll. We can't pay you a dime."

Fuck.

I took a breath.

"That's ridiculous," I said. "Both of you saw what I brought to the table that night in girls and the guest list! You can't just leave me hanging like this."

They leaned together in whispered conversation.

"All right," Roger said at last. "We're going to pay you what we were going to pay the promoter and Dilon that night—300 dollars. We'll deal with them later. I know it's not the 1,200 you were promised, but it's better than nothing. Thanks for selling some tables and helping out."

I watched Roger write me a check. Three hundred dollars. Three hundred dollars wouldn't get you shit in a club, but if I worked in this industry, I could get anything there for free. It wasn't even a payment on my car, but the money wasn't the point. I was trying to get a toehold to start a life in LA.

That's it? This is the end? Nope—you've already come this far, Eli. You aren't going to walk away that quickly. Use that secret weapon of yours—your mouth.

"Roger," I pleaded, "I badly need a job. Please give me the opportunity to work with you and your team!"

"Sorry, man. I don't have the funds, and in all honesty, I have no idea who you are or what you're really about. I just met you."

"Give me a chance, man! I'm not going to steal money from the door. I'm an honest and trustworthy guy. You can count on me.

Give me one single shot—I promise I won't let you down! There has got to be something I can do! I really need a job—just give me one time!"

They whispered to each other for a moment.

"Look, man, we honestly don't have the budget to pay you to promote," Roger said. "Plus, we need a more experienced and local promoter before we even think about adding anyone new to our team. But you seem genuine, and we get that you're a hard worker.

"We actually do need someone we trust to run the guest list at the door—somebody who doesn't know anybody. It only pays a hundred dollars per night. Your main focus is to make sure that nobody slips in who isn't on that list, and keeping track of who came in with what promoter. We'll deal with the rest."

It wasn't much money, but I instantly knew this gig would be my gateway to meeting, connecting, and networking with the city's tastemakers. I'd be greeting every single person who walked through those red velvet ropes. Roger and Jake sensed my energy, and energy doesn't lie.

"Done deal!" I nearly shouted. "When do I start?"

That moment would change my life forever.

Friday night I was back at the club, clipboard in hand, dressed for success in a black pea coat, a button-down shirt, and a fierce grin. That first night was really exciting. I greeted every person who came in, and quickly saw that working the door gave me a chance to connect with celebrities and everyone else who came into the club. It was better than being on the floor inside. When I talked with someone I thought I should know—because I spoke with everyone—I made sure to introduce myself.

I was excited, determined, and grateful to be on my way.

I got the job done every week, and after a month Roger asked me to run the Tuesday guest list at another club called Falcon, right off Sunset Boulevard. A month after that, another guy at Kress, Baron, asked me to help run the ropes for the Saturday nights he promoted there. Roger had spoken highly of me and, boom, that was that. Within a couple of months, I was running the door and guest lists three nights a week at two clubs.

I was gaining momentum. I was gaining respect. I was gaining traction.

But my relationship with Melissa, who I had brought to Kress that first night, was on the rocks.

I had started dating her when I was seventeen and she was twenty-two. She was five years older and intrigued the hell out of me: a beautiful Italian with long brown hair, bright green eyes, and a magnificently toned body. And get this—she was an elementary substitute teacher by day, and a stripper by night.

I thought that was fucking awesome. (My parents didn't, though.)

The truth was, she and I didn't really understand the basics of being in a boyfriend-girlfriend relationship. I thought I was in love.

That meant she was able to hurt me—maybe more than I should have let her. She was beautiful, and I was head-over-heels for her, but she didn't make the best choices for our relationship—stripping, for one thing. Word was she was doing more than stripping. Plus her old boyfriend seemed to be hanging out with her an awful lot. Her MySpace had crazy pictures of her half-naked on it. One day she came home from teaching middle school and said that one of the students had her picture as a screen saver on his phone, although she tried to deny it was her (she had taken to wearing a wig at school, trying to alter her image, which was kind of ridiculous and definitely not effective).

I never actually caught Melissa cheating, but I suspected she lied to me. A lot. I had never been hurt like this by someone I thought I loved. The pressure to do something, to get out of this pain and hurt, built up inside me. I was going to explode. After three years, shortly after that date at Kress, I finally ended things. I knew she was not girlfriend material anymore. The emotional ups and downs were wracking me, and I knew I needed to get through the heartbreak and move on.

I had tried to break up with her before, but each time she broke down crying and begging for another chance. I don't like conflict and confrontation, so I lost my nerve. This happened twice. The third time I didn't break up in person—I called her. She cried and begged, but I knew I had to ignore her, and I did. That was my first relationship, and the last time we spoke.

Melissa taught me something important—something that would serve me well in the world of nightlife I was entering. She taught me to have thick skin and a firm backbone. These are two characteristics I truly would need to succeed in the Hollywood nightclub world.

THREE

HOUSE OF PLAY

"You become what you surround yourself with. Energies are contagious. Choose carefully."

—ANONYMOUS

I SETTLED INTO A NIGHTLY ROUTINE AT KRESS. I PARKED my black Chrysler 300 in a paid lot a block away, walked to work, and put in my time making sure the right people got in and had a great evening. I liked working nights, and after about 12:30 or 1 a.m., I got a second wind. I'd find myself wide awake and wondering what else the warm Los Angeles night held when I clocked out around 1:45 in the morning.

As I walked back through the alley toward my car, I sometimes saw recognizable A-list celebrities being escorted discretely into a back door. I knew this door—it led into an outrageously popular club called Playhouse. Of course, I heard all the buzz about Playhouse. It made me curious, and seeing faces I recognized from the trades and Instagram slipping through the dark and into its secretive interior made me only more curious.

The word was out—this place was *hot*. It was *the* spot, having its blazing moment in the fickle light of nightlife fame. Name an artist, actor, or massive DJ who was out on the town, and you could be certain they were hosting, performing, or partying there.

I had to get in.

What was all the fuss about? What could be so great, so unworldly, inside Playhouse that we didn't have at Kress? Getting those answers became my mission. Kress was great, but I was on a journey to move up in the world. Clearly, Playhouse, a block away from Kress, was the next step, waiting for me to climb it.

I had some cards to play. Not a lot, but more than I'd had a few months earlier, when I was a naïve kid from Moreno Valley. I still had that kid's bravado and willingness to try to talk my way past anyone and into anything.

One evening after work I didn't walk down the alley to my car. I walked down the street, confident and resolute, right up to the girl managing the front door. I knew her name was Allison. She was slim and blonde, with beautiful green eyes.

"Hey, Allison," I said, friendly as I could be. "My name's Eli. I work at a few venues around town running doors and guest lists. I've been wanting to check this place out—I've heard nothing but amazing things. If you ever want to come by where I work, I'll make sure you're taken care of."

She looked at me like I'd just taken a shit on the sidewalk. Her sidewalk. She gave exactly zero fucks about my you-scratch-my-back-I'll-scratch-yours pitch. She didn't even say anything to me, just looked me up and down, then turned away.

Now, someone like Allison is exactly the kind of person you want running your door if you own a club. What she did was correct— otherwise, she's not keeping it *right and tight*. She can't let in anyone who comes up and offers to trade favors. She can't be open to being bribed by people palming bills. She was strict, fierce, and not opening those velvet ropes.

So it was the right thing for her to do for the club owners. It was the wrong thing for her to do as far as my plan to get in was concerned.

"What a bitch," I mumbled.

"Excuse me?"

She had read my lips. "I heard you. There is no way you are ever coming through these doors as long as I'm out here."

Well, fuck, Eli. Good move.

This was not going exactly to plan.

I had just made a hard thing a hundred times harder for myself. I had let my emotions get the better of me for a moment, and I was paying the price. But this was not the first time I had tried to get into a nightclub I'd never been to. There had to be an alternative way in that got me around Allison.

Never give up.

I saw a guy in a suit talking to the staff and smoking a cigarette in the shadows near the front door. I thought he might be one of the managers, so I struck up a conversation with him.

I am blessed with a very good ability to read people almost instantly, getting a sense of their personality and what they want. As soon as I began talking to Rod, a middle-aged Irishman, I sensed he was a great guy. We connected. I explained what I wanted and how Allison had shut me down. I offered to take care of him if he ever wanted to step around the corner and check out Kress. I was as genuine as I could be, and I could tell he was one of those guys who could read people really well, too. I knew he was sizing me up.

"Okay, cool," he said as our conversation wound down. "I hear you. Come back tomorrow and I'll take care of you."

As I turned toward my car, I saw Allison arguing with him. She had heard the whole conversation and knew he had overridden her decision. She was furious, but I was thinking, "Looks like Rod calls the shots!"

The next night I got over to Playhouse as soon as work at Kress wrapped up, speed walking the block to their door. Rod let me in and showed me around the space. Playhouse lived up to the hype. On one level was a live trumpet act, on another a live DJ. Aerial dancers gyrated in the space, hung from the ceiling.

"If you need anything, just let me know," he said, and turned me loose.

I saw A-listers I recognized all over the place, and beautiful people packed the floors wall-to-wall. Most interesting to me was a small performance stage that contained two small tables for guests to get up close and personal with the artist or DJ working there.

Nightclubs are about psychology, particularly about power and pecking order. That's why they make it hard to get into one in the first place. Think about it—you are trying to give them money, literally begging at the velvet ropes to be let in, and the team there is turning you away!

That seems like a strange way to run a business, doesn't it? Why would they do that?

Because nightclubs are about exclusivity. Exclusivity is about status. And status is something that we, like all primates, crave deeply. That exclusivity is maintained by the people who hold power—the owners, the hosts, the door staff—who get to approve you or, more likely, diss you. Everything about a nightclub is rooted in our human craving for external validation—for someone else to tell us we're pretty enough, cool enough, hot enough, rich enough.

That's not just the currency that runs nightclubs—it's the currency of Hollywood and of the entire entertainment industry. As a culture we like to celebrate the iconoclast, the outsider, the visionary who went their own way. But what we actually crave as individuals is other people's approval, and nowhere is this truer than in the seething belly of Hollywood, California. Hollywood is all about "being chosen"—being chosen to be represented, being chosen for the part, being chosen for the shoot, being chosen for the voice, being chosen for the look, being chosen for the date. It's all about somebody else telling us we are worthy.

Nightclubs are built on this primal human hunger.

Getting into a club is only the beginning. Inside a club is a complex, dynamic dance for status that is both different and the same every night. Where are you standing? Who are you with? Do you have a table? Who is at your table? Whose table can you join? Who wants to join your table? And on and on.

The stage at Playhouse was a very, very coveted space. A bouncer stood guard over a velvet rope at the bottom of a short flight of stairs, taking direction from a team member running the stage above. People approached in a steady stream, trying to talk their way onto that stage. Like the dais at an ancient Roman feast, it was the place where you could be above the crowd, a place to see and, more importantly, to be seen. That's where you'd find the club owners, the DJs, the A-listers. It was a place where you were manifestly, demonstrably, and visibly at the top of the pecking order. You showed you had the highest status.

Whoever ran that velvet rope held a lot of power inside that club, and had a lot to do with how well guests' evenings went.

Over the next few weeks, I became a regular at Playhouse on Friday and Saturday nights, coming in with girlfriends and colleagues from Kress. I got to know Rod a bit better, and saw that he knew a lot about how to operate a club, which depends in no small part on knowing human psychology and handling conflict, things he excelled at. The club was owned by a trio of Russians who had been in the business for years. Like most Russians I've met, these guys fit the pattern: they either love you or hate you, and if you're dealing with them, you'd better hope they love you, because otherwise you're in for a hell of a ride. They knew everyone, and they had a good reputation. With one call they could blacklist you from working again.

Rod introduced me first to Ivan, who always dressed casually, shaved his head clean, wore tiny glasses, and cracked a steady stream of jokes as he spent his evenings keeping an eye on who and what made it inside his building. He was funny—he liked to tell people he found me wandering on Hollywood Boulevard wearing an Affliction t-shirt, square-toed boots, and a bedazzled studded belt. If Ivan saw that you showed up with beautiful women or celebrities, he'd take care of you. The formula for good business in nightclubs, after all, starts with hot women and A-list stars.

"Eli's a good kid," Rod had murmured to Ivan, and that endorsement meant that pretty soon Ivan and I were hanging out on Friday and Saturday evenings, often at the foot of that little stage, where Ivan and the bouncer controlled who got up into that rar-efied air. He struggled to keep it *right and tight*. He seemed not to know exactly what sort of rules he wanted to maintain. He couldn't manage it alone, and he didn't want to.

Create a position for yourself, Eli. Be different.

I can do this for you, I started to tell him. I know the right people. I can make this work better than it's working right now.

Ivan had three other partners: Viktor, Dimitri, and Alexander. Viktor was the main investor in the club, a guy in his forties who looked every part the Russian mobster. He was strictly focused on making money, but he had a warm heart toward me and helped me out a ton as time went on, always pumping me up as "our guy."

I liked Dimitri in particular. He was the youngest of the three, a little scruffy, casually dressed, and talking shit to me all the time but actually having my back and steering me the right way. He was in his twenties and had a way with the ladies, which was fun to be a part of.

Alexander was Russian and Armenian, always dressed in a suit and a tight buzz-cut, in his thirties.

The partners and Rod agreed to give me a shot. We didn't talk about money—we didn't have to. I was going to be in charge of running the stage at the hottest, hippest nightclub in LA. I was confident they would take care of me, and I was pumped to have made a huge step up on my journey.

This was my cue to leave Kress. Standing at the foot of that stage, I would have huge opportunities to network, grow my personal brand, and elevate myself.

So on a Friday night in October 2009, I showed up at Playhouse in a pair of tight black slacks, a button-down shirt, and a black necktie. My head was shaved clean, a statement of maturity and power. I was prepared for battle, ready to make it happen for myself, for the guests and for the club.

Nobody on the floor staff seemed to know what I was doing at the stage, but I didn't care. I had a job to do, and I only answered to Rod and Ivan. I didn't have much direction from them, and I didn't need it. I knew what I had to do.

Tunnel vision, Eli. Time to get creative and hold it down.

The night's theme was "Dirty. Sexy. House." Lights began flashing, the aerial dancers began spinning, the house music built up. Hundreds of people filled the floor and pushed toward the stage.

My stage.

This was where I would build my reputation and brand. It was my palette for painting my career success. I put my hand on the velvet rope and took my place as a player in the dark, pulsating world I was making my own.

I knew I was on trial. I was on a steep learning curve about Playhouse, its ins and outs and internal politics. I had to crush this new role, or I would be crushed. My job was to create structure that would benefit the stage and the venue. My first priority was to host and care for whatever celebrity, artist, or notable DJ that was booked or spinning that night. Every one of these people had a "rider" attached to their performance contract, a specific set of requests for food and beverages. I made sure I was always on point about delivering these. Some performers really took advantage of this, asking for thousand-dollar bottles of "1942" tequila, or bottles of Dom Perignon, or Armand de Brignac Ace of Spades Rose Champagne that we sold for a couple thousand dollars apiece. Others wanted pizza or Mexican food, knowing that the owners had invested in late-night restaurants right outside the club's front door.

If they were happy, the club was happy, the owners were happy, and ultimately I would thrive. Doing this work meant that I had a chance to build a relationship with every VIP who performed on that stage—guys like DJ Tiesto and Chris Brown. I had the opportunity to create a personal brand by connecting with each of them.

Be genuine, be you, earn respect and gain their trust.

My next priority was enforcing the owners' list of who could and could not be on the stage. I worked closely with a beefy security guard who managed the foot of the stairs. He'd do what I told him to, but nevertheless most nights were stressful and sweaty. Clients, promoters, and celebrities would cluster in front of the guard, waving to get my attention from the stage, begging for permission to come up. Functionally, I was a VIP doorman for the most exclusive spot inside the club. I had to follow protocol and keep it *right and tight*.

You're not likely to find many sober people inside a nightclub. Most of my encounters were with people who were drunk, high or just out of their minds, so there was a fair bit of arguing and yelling. Situations that could easily be diffused among sober people in the daylight often escalated under the throbbing conditions of a nightclub. Often when I said "no" to someone it set them off, especially in the late, addled hours of the night. That's just how things were, and how they always will be in a nightclub. I couldn't take any of the abuse or pressure personally—it just came with the job. I had to let go of emotional reactions and stress, remembering that most of the people I was dealing with were in their own worlds, so high that no matter how I communicated with them they wouldn't comprehend and likely would be upset.

After two weeks in this role, I began to hear people referring to me as "the stage manager." That was fine by me.

Most club staff would have a few shots during a night, taking the edge off to make the night a little more enjoyable, a little easier to deal with the belligerent drunks and druggies they encountered. Not me. At least not when I was working. I wanted to stay focused.

It was a friend's kindness that got me in trouble.

Chris lived not far from Playhouse, and he opened his apartment to me during my trial run. He was a mysterious guy. No one seemed to know what he did—he always seemed to have one story or another—but he was connected with people. This was a godsend—I wouldn't have to jet the seventy miles home after a long, late-night shift. Chris was a good guy, tall and slim with a distinctive Mohawk, known and liked in the nightclub world. I was more than happy to crash at his place.

I worked for four straight weeks, Thursday through Saturday nights, with no indications from the owners about what my job was or what, if anything, I was being paid. They finally agreed to pay me $400 per week to cover those nights. Okay, not great money—but in my mind, the money wasn't the point. I was becoming a success as the stage manager at Playhouse, and that was setting me up for bigger successes.

I could wait on the money, but there was no way to put aside the stress I felt every night. I put enormous pressure on myself to be excellent at my job of managing boozing, drugged-up, raging people who all wanted something from me, all wanted access to that stage, all were pushing, pushing, pushing. And all around me, from the clientele to the performers to the club staff, people were partying. Everyone was drinking, and everyone wanted me to drink, too.

"Have one drink," they said. "Take the edge off. It's the end of the night, you don't have to drive. Let loose."

You are a reflection of who you surround yourself with. Really, could it have happened any differently?

It was only a matter of time before I caved.

I intended to keep it clean. But now that I didn't have to drive home—it was only a short walk to Chris's place—that iron-clad resolution started to erode. My drink of choice, handed up from the bar below the stage, was a sugar-free Red Bull and vodka. So began my slow, inexorable journey down the booze hole—which in time would lead to other, worse holes.

Alcohol gave me a release. Instead of going to Chris's and going to sleep after work, I stayed out. I went to after-parties and after-after-parties. I felt amazing, on top of the world. Felt like I'd solved all my problems with a bottle and a glass. I looked around and concluded, perhaps not entirely correctly, that everybody important in the nightclub business was drinking and doing drugs. Now I was, too. I was part of the popular crew, and it made me feel great. They were cool, what they were doing was cool, and since I was doing it now, that made me cool, too, right?

The feeling was amazing.

That's what I told myself. But the truth is that misery loves company. I just didn't see it that way at the time.

If someone is going to an after-party following a night at a club, it's likely they are an alcoholic, a drug addict, trying to get laid or just generally out of their minds. I chose to overlook that because I saw my job as networking and connecting. These parties were another playing field upon which I could do that. The more people I knew, the more contacts I had, the more connected I was in the city, the more value I added to the Eli Wehbe brand. That was what would get me to the next level—because there is always a next level in this game.

As the months passed, the hole got deeper.

Every alcohol, every party drug you can think of (and some you probably can't) is available in the nightclub world. Somebody always knows somebody who can get whatever you want. That's just the way it is. I had my fair share: cocaine, ecstasy, GHB, molly, Xanax, acid, ketamine, magic mushrooms, and DMT. You name the party drug, and I've probably used it or personally abused it.

Taking drugs and drinking was easy to rationalize. I wanted to connect with people. I wanted them to be real with me. They needed to be able to relate to me. If I was the sober one in a group of drugged-up addicts or drunks, I was the outcast. I was telegraphing that I was the guy who was *better* than them. Who wants that guy around?

I told myself that to make connections I had to be accepted, and to be accepted I had to do what everyone was doing around me. This was a deep, black pit of rationalization, dark and strange. I dove into it with no shovel to get myself back out. As I saw things, a life of partying was a life that was richer and better. If you weren't part of that world, you were missing out. Why would I choose to do that?

Unavoidably, I became a reflection of the people I surrounded myself with, which meant I was high pretty much all the time— especially on cocaine. I really liked cocaine; it kept me alert and entertained and wanting to make connections for hours, sometimes for days, bending the ears of anyone and everyone I met, all while enjoying the high of a lifetime. My job was turning into a never-ending party in which I was always high, making money, meeting people.

Living the dream.

That's what I told myself, anyway. All of this made me look more and more successful in my role as stage manager at Playhouse. I seemed to know everyone. I began booking high-end clients for tables and bottle service. People who mattered knew who I was; I was becoming the go-to guy at Playhouse, and so long as I kept the stage tight and on-point, nobody cared if I was high or drunk. I just had to do my job.

Success is a funny thing. Everyone in Hollywood grasps for it, yet when you achieve it—if you achieve it—it's not what you thought. In my case, my success as stage manager started to attract envy and resentment, particularly from one of the club's Russian partners, Alexander. He wanted to be the face of Playhouse, to live in the spotlight, but he didn't have the skills to be good at that. This made him angry, bitter, envious. He watched me from the club's shadows, taking in my success, and I think it made him crazy. He'd come up on the stage and bust my balls in front of everyone for no reason, just because he could.

I was getting ready to head out after another baller Thursday night when Alexander pulled me aside. "Eli, this will be your last night working here," he said. "We won't be needing you anymore.

I've spoken to my partners, and we've all agreed that you know too many people now. You're partying excessively and letting way too many of your new friends up on stage. We've hired somebody who knows nobody and can keep the stage scene tight."

Then, like he was doing me a favor, he added, "You can still book tables and make a commission on what you send in—but this is the end of your stage manager position."

He was right about one thing: I did know too many people, which was making running the stage more difficult. I had to say no to people whose positive opinion I valued, and I didn't want to jeopardize those relationships. That was a tricky situation for me, as I could start to undo all of the goodwill and connections I had been building. And yes, I was a raging partier on the job—but I was doing a good job. I was running things the way our protocol said I should run them.

What have I really done wrong? This can't be the end. I'm just getting momentum. I'm on a roll!

I begged Alexander to let me stay, but he didn't give a shit. There was going to be no discussion. Something didn't smell right.

I called Ivan and Dimitri. They had no idea what Alexander was talking about.

"Just take the weekend off and come to the club Monday night, we'll work it out," they said.

When I showed up, Dimitri said, "Look, ignore what Alexander said. You're going to report to Ivan and me. If there's one thing I've learned about you, it's that you're a hard worker and a great host, so we're moving you to running the floor. You're going to table-touch all the clients, and you can share a table with Ivan and me to host any of your guests. This will suit you much better than the stage, I promise."

You're wrong. I created that stage manager role! I belong there!

That's what I thought in the moment, but Dimitri was right. As the floor host, I worked in a suit and tie, visiting with every table and making sure that everyone who had bought a table was having a great time, spending a lot of money, and excited about coming back. I got to know every inch of the club and got close with all the staff.

Alexander couldn't stop his partners from putting me in this role, so he was just rude to me. I became the right-hand man for the partners, and built more and more relationships with clients. Anytime an A-list actor, artist or influencer walked through the front door, I got a call or text, and was there to show them their table and take care of them. I got to know people like ball players from the LA Dodgers, Jenny McCarthy, Leah Remini, and many others.

Pretty soon, the big spenders started calling me directly to book their tables. They referred their friends, too. It wasn't long before I was making more commission money on table sales than anyone else at Playhouse. I was booking the majority of the money being spent. If some guy I brought in dropped $30,000, I could walk home with $5,000 for the night.

Cha-ching!

Even though I was making bank, it wasn't about the money. It was about building my brand.

By 2013, three years after that evening when I had talked Rod into letting me slide in the front door past Allison, I had become a very public face at Playhouse. The nightlife business is all about what you bring to the table. At first, people resent a newcomer. They might think, "This guy's on my territory, he's taking money or status or power from me." But if you produced, when you start really bringing it, they see how you are helping everyone. Allison and I actually became good friends, which is sort of funny when you look at how we started off. Allison respected me for what I was doing for the club—everyone did.

Many people assumed, incorrectly, that I was a partner in the club. People could believe what they wanted about my success, because if that story was out there about me being a Playhouse partner, all that did was set me up for my next step up in the industry. I was climbing the ladder of life, and that was all that mattered.

Hollywood must be where they came up with the phrase "fake it 'til you make it," and I was all about that. Let me be clear: I didn't lie to people. One of the ways I set myself apart from the mass of operators, hangers-on, and wannabes was that I played it straight. I was honest with people to the point of being blunt. But if they wanted to make assumptions about me, I let them create their own story. That's what they were going to do anyway. Certainly, I projected a very curated image. I made sure to play the part I wanted to have, even if I didn't quite have it yet. If you saw me then, you can be sure I was driving a Mercedes, wearing a Rolex and the hottest designer shoes and clothes, and had a gorgeous model by my side.

I wanted to keep people guessing. I wanted them envious. I wanted them to wonder how I had pulled this off, how I had gone from nothing to *something*. I had a huge work ethic around staying in the public eye and keeping everyone guessing.

In fact, I was making money. The money was a tool to help me keep climbing toward my vision of having my own club. If I made enough to pay my bills, buy a Rolex, drive a nice car, and live the lifestyle I wanted to live, then I was building my brand and doing what I needed to do.

After a couple of years at Playhouse, I realized something about money. I hung out with a lot of very, very wealthy guys, and I saw that *they* wanted what *I* had. They might be very successful, but they wanted my lifestyle. They wanted to be in the environment I was in. They wanted to hook up with the girls I was hooking up with. Once I understood that, I knew that I needed to keep doing what I was doing.

The feeling was amazing.

But chasing more achievement, however you measure it, can be a form of addiction no different than chasing alcohol or drugs or sex. When getting more money or success or achievement makes you want more, how is that any different from being an alcoholic looking for the next fix?

Los Angeles is full of beautiful, shallow people with terrible personalities who feed this addiction to material success. In 2013, I was very busy trying to impress just those people. I know now that broken people love impressing broken people. No successful person cares about others' material possessions. They care about what actually matters in life: is someone down to earth, genuine, loyal, intelligent, trustworthy? Or no depth? Then no interest. Yes, there are good, genuine people in LA and in the nightlife world, as there are anywhere. But they are as hard to find as a white cat in a snowstorm.

Around this time I found Instagram to be a very effective tool for building my personal brand. It was taking off as one of the first big social media apps, and was the easiest way to promote my life and attract more business. By promoting my lifestyle, I was attracting people who would want to come to the club. Long-term, I wanted people who would follow me for who I am, but I wasn't there yet. I needed to build my brand, but I hadn't established myself in a meaningful way. So I posted and tagged with celebrities and influencers and models, showing my lifestyle, the fancy cars, the fancy clothes, the beautiful people. I don't believe that any individual is better than any other individual, but it was my job to celebrate the brands, the DJs, the rappers—whoever would bring in more business.

In 2013, the California streetwear brand Pink Dolphin approached me to help with marketing. I only had about 20,000 followers, but they included a lot of influencers and celebrities, and Pink Dolphin wanted that reach. They hired me to use my connections to get influencers to wear their clothing or participate in photo shoots for the company. I already knew many, many influencers and was able to get many of them to participate, wearing Pink Dolphin and tagging the brand on Instagram, Snapchat, and Twitter. This cross-promotion from nightlife into streetwear grew my following and my personal brand even faster than before. The bigger my brand became, the more connected I became, the sooner I was going to own my own nightclub.

My work with Pink Dolphin fit into my personal belief that the more I could do for others, the more power I had. A more cynical way to look at this was, "If you can't be used, you're useless." That was a dark truth about Los Angeles, one I saw play out every day. In the nightclub business, you are only as good as your last night. You could have a hundred good nights for the club, but one bad night and you could be out. People might give you an opportunity, but they wouldn't help you out. As soon as people sensed that a promoter wasn't valuable, wasn't connected to the right people, he became useless to them. It could happen really fast—a few bad nights and that promoter could be out of a job.

Because of that, I worked relentlessly to stay connected, to stay relevant, to stay on top of who was who and what was happening. My phone was my business, and I worked it constantly. I could barely bring myself to leave Los Angeles for even a weekend— what might I miss? When I did, I was on my screen constantly.

Yes, it was work, but I actually liked helping the people around me. I enjoyed being able to give value—it made me feel good. And I didn't have the desire to ask other people to do me favors. I worked hard to achieve what I did, and I wanted to continue to feel that I didn't owe anyone.

Keep on grinding, baby.

FOUR

YOUR EGO IS NOT YOUR AMIGO

"Some beautiful paths can't be discovered without getting lost."

—ERROL OZAN

W HEN A NIGHTCLUB IS HOT, IT CAN BE A FANTASTIC ride. Like all rides, it will eventually end. A club might be hot for two years, then some other club will become the "in" place to be, and the energy will shift. Club success depends on four main ingredients: newness, who is operating it, which promoters are working there, and who the clientele is.

By late 2014 I had been enjoying a long, beautiful ride at Playhouse for five years, grinding away every night like I owned the place. Amazingly, we were still doing well. Playhouse made Los Angeles history with such a long, profitable run as a hot location, even with newer venues like 1 Oak, Warwick, and Hyde competing against us. We were not the very hottest club anymore, but we still brought in the A-listers, and you'd find a cool crowd on any given night. We booked huge electronic dance music (EDM) DJs and A-list artists, and our numbers continued to rock the bottom line.

I worked as if I had invested all my money and half my blood into that club. This is not normal in the Hollywood nightclub business, which is characterized by zero loyalty. Most promoters and hosts jump from club to club based on what they think is best for them in that moment.

I had a different MO. When it came to working at Playhouse, I was all in, every night. Hate it or love it, that's who I am.

By this point I was a hot commodity in the nightclub world. I was a master at bringing in business and getting people to spend money. Whenever a shiny, new club was preparing to open, I knew I would hear from someone who wanted to lure me away from Playhouse to work in what they promised was going to be the latest, best, hottest destination.

I always declined, always politely. Viktor, Ivan, Dimitri, and Rod had given me my big break in the cold, hard world of nightlife, and they had my back. So I had theirs.

For a year, we had been talking on and off about bringing me into the partnership, but we hadn't come to any conclusion. There wasn't any urgency, any excitement about bringing me in. Maybe that was for the best, because as I looked back over Playhouse's long run, I knew it couldn't last. This club wasn't going to be at or near the top forever, maybe not even for much longer. More and more nights catered to a less-exclusive crowd that wasn't my scene. The club was changing, and I began to feel stagnant.

In the fall of 2014, I began spending my evenings at Warwick, a club that had opened on Sunset Boulevard a year earlier. It was a two-story, modern lounge featuring bottle service, a stellar mixology program, and some of the hottest bartenders in the business. Plus, there was a strong entertainment component with talented DJs. The vibe was refined and unpretentious yet beautiful and comfortable. Warwick had a reputation as one of the most awe-inspiring and exclusive clubs in the city.

Warwick

On my nights off I'd drop into Warwick with some celebrities or hot women, and even when I was working at Playhouse, I'd start the evening at Warwick. Everyone on the inside team—that is, the people who were on duty every night—had been there since the opening. The owners wanted me to work for them, which was a big deal—I'd be the first person on that team who hadn't been part of the founding group, which operated like a close-knit family.

At last, the operating partners and I came to an agreement. I was excited, but I am a loyal person. I couldn't just walk out on the Playhouse partners.

I sat down with Ivan, Dimitri, and Viktor and came to a friendly agreement. The fact was, I was getting too expensive for them. My commission fees were higher than they wanted to pay. They knew, too, that I needed to grow. It was time for me to move on. We left on good terms, and we remain friends to this day. That was an important accomplishment for me—I don't like to burn bridges. If Kress got me off the launchpad, Playhouse's owners launched me into orbit in the universe I so desired. As I turned toward the next stage of my journey, I felt—and still feel—nothing but gratitude toward them.

All that was left for me to nail down my new role at Warwick was to meet with Benjamin, the majority investor at the club. It was my big job interview.

So what did I do?

I stayed up the entire night before on a massive alcohol-and-blow-fueled bender. Early the next morning, suited up in black from head to toe, operating on no sleep and still really high, I showed up at Benjamin's office.

Cocky? You bet I was. Foolish? Yeah, that too.

But I pulled it off beautifully. Benjamin was a sharp, witty, no-bullshit older gentleman, yet he had no idea that as I sat in his office I was out of my damn mind. I kept it laser-sharp with him.

"Welcome to the Warwick family, Eli," he finally said, and the meeting was over. I'd pulled it off. And I knew what I was in for.

Stay in your lane. Stick to the plan. Don't get emotional. Stick to the vision. You are going to own a club by the time you are twenty-eight! Onward and upward, it's the only direction to go. You got this!

The new thing was like the old thing: I did what I do best. My role as in-house host was similar to my last role at Playhouse. My biggest strength is that I am a consummate people person. After more than five years in the business in the heart of Hollywood, I had a monster list of people at my fingertips—people like Kevin Hart, Justin Bieber, and Paris Hilton. Think of your favorite pop stars, rappers, athletes, models, comedians, and influencers from this time period, and I promise you I knew them. I was bringing them in, too.

I had my own table where I could host friends, clients, celebs, and women. I took pride in curating a lively, fun atmosphere that ensured people came back for more. Which they did.

My job was to party. There was always an after-party—some guy who had dropped $20,000 and was renting an Airbnb in Bel Air or Beverly Hills. He'd invite everyone, send out the address, and we'd all show up at his crib and keep going. I was paid to do this.

Sounds great, doesn't it?

I used that "fact" to go deep down the hole.

I only party for social reasons, and my job is to be social. I only party if I want to enjoy the night with people who came out to see me. I party to network. Never party for any other reason, Eli.

This was a brilliant strategy for fooling myself. I was able to tell myself I did not have an addiction to drugs or alcohol, yet I consumed drugs and alcohol every night because that was my "job." Sure, I was drinking booze and doing hard drugs, but that's how I connected with the "right" individuals. I'd have a few drinks, do a few lines, and be ready to stay up well into the wee hours, talking nonsense to someone I wanted to connect with because they had joined the party, too.

In those moments, I could step out of myself sometimes and sense how surreal all of this was. Yet it also felt so good, so right. Of course, that was just the drugs talking. Drugs and alcohol clouded my mind to what was real in my relationships, even as I thought they were helping me make more legitimate, deeper connections. I spent many, many late nights talking for hours with people who were similarly out of their minds. I called them "family," and I thought of them like that. I convinced myself that they were good, close friends who would never turn on me in any way.

Of course that was bullshit. It took me a long time to figure this out, but the "family" I snorted and popped and drank with were almost all the same people who talked shit about me (or anybody else) as soon as my back was turned. They wouldn't speak to me if they realized I didn't have anything to offer them—I was useless if I couldn't be used.

* * *

My social media following continued to grow, and one influencer in particular caught my eye, a twenty-year-old brunette bombshell from Texas named Dakota. I slid up in her DMs and asked if she would like some free Pink Dolphin gear.

She did, and as I'd hoped she would, she posted pictures of herself in the gear and tagged Pink Dolphin and me. Recognition like this was a primary way for me to grow my personal brand, so I thanked her directly. We began to message each other. Then we began to talk, conversations full of wit and sarcasm and laughter. Within a few months we were in nearly constant conversation: Facetime, DMs, texts. We became best friends before we ever actually saw each other in person.

Dakota was different. I learned she had a huge heart, deeply-felt moral grounding, and a commitment to animals and the environment. More interesting to me was that she didn't seem to want to know me because of my status or my connections or what I could do for her. She wanted to know me for, well, me. She came across as truly genuine.

She was my unicorn.

She wanted to come visit LA. Both of us were excited by the prospect of meeting, but her primary objective was to check out a work opportunity and see about moving to the city. I had never met anyone like her in LA, and I wanted to have her back. Los Angeles can be toxic and destructive, a place that breaks dreams—especially the dreams of wide-eyed transplants from other places.

Dakota had the potential to make it here, I knew that. She was clearly smart. But she also was young, gullible, and naïve. I could give her a head start that could make the difference between making and breaking it, but she still would have to learn some hard lessons here on her own.

There's a reason most people who move here don't succeed. Most transplants are running away from something—small-town America, rural life, a family they don't like, something they are ashamed of. They come to LA to live out the American myth of reinventing themselves. They think they can be whatever they want here—and it's true, a few of them can and will. But most can't and don't, and a big reason is that they did not bring their Big City Survival Kit: thick skin, the ability to convince people (what I call "a good mouth"), emotional control, and a plan to earn their stripes. The truth is, LA doesn't like you. It doesn't owe you anything.

Even though I'm from Southern California, I'm still an outsider. Moreno Valley might as well be Kansas as far as Hollywood is concerned. I heard plenty of transplants talk shit about LA, but I never did. Most of the really negative experiences transplants have come at the hands of other transplants. I'm not saying Hollywood natives are all sweetness and light, but the worst experiences transplants have seemed to come from others like them. It is shitty people meeting shitty people.

That can break you if you're not tough. A lot of kids in their teens and twenties show up with dreams but find themselves on a bus or a plane home a lot sooner than they imagined—and not covered in glory, either. No matter what I did for Dakota, the hard way would be the only way. Welcome to Hollywood.

Dakota was going to arrive in mid-December of 2014. She and I had no official plan to meet up, and I definitely was going to play it cool. I clearly liked her, but I wasn't going to be the guy who made it weird. I valued our best friend status. She would have to make the first move, and she did.

"So are you going to ask me out to dinner or what" read the text.

Bingo.

"Oh yeah? You're asking me to take you to dinner? That's a first, but of course I will, let's do it!"

When I picked her up on her first night in the city, our eyes locked, and the spark lit.

We both blurted out, "So, do I look like my photos?" We agreed we looked better than our photos.

Dakota had light brown eyes filled with mystery and wisdom, smooth brown hair, and the face and body of a goddess. Before that evening she already knew a lot about me: my addictions, my insecurities, my OCD, my ADD, my routines, my past. If you can think about it, we already had talked about it.

That first night we had dinner with a couple of my friends in West Hollywood at an Italian restaurant I liked. She stopped by my house the following night to say goodbye, and then was back to Texas. Nothing had happened between us, yet everything had. We both knew we were really into the other. The energy between us kicked up a notch, and our conversations changed.

Before we began dating, she filled my days with bright light and positive energy. She was an old soul, wise beyond her years, spiritual, emotionally strong. She had the wisdom and experience I would expect from someone much older.

It was funny—we tend to think that wisdom comes from experience, but I had seen pretty much the opposite in the nightclub business. Most of the older people I knew were anything but wise or mature. They sought validation from all the wrong sources and clogged their heads with drugs and alcohol. They focused on the next bit of bling they wanted, the next material proof of their success, the next guy or girl they wanted to bang.

Was I becoming like that? Was that how others were starting to see me?

Dakota was a gift sent by the universe, someone to teach me lessons, elevate me, help me grow. She might be young, but she would be a teacher for me. That's how I saw her almost from the start, and I was profoundly grateful for this unicorn.

We made it official in Las Vegas in early January, on her twenty-first birthday. I went out to see her at a club where she had a gig to host, and we began dating. I heard that dating your best friend could be amazing, but I'd never had the chance. Now I did.

She asked me things that opened up my mind. She didn't want to talk about work or business, she wanted to understand my personality and soul. She wasn't afraid to talk about what she believed in, and she was passionate about animals, and a committed vegan. (When we went out to eat, she never judged or pressured me to stop eating meat, but sometimes she'd say, "You know, this is better.")

Los Angeles is a small town in some ways, where people date around and everyone knows everyone else. It was a huge thing for me to have someone no one knew, and who had no baggage. She showed me a lot of genuine attention that was about me, not about my status. That was new, and I appreciated it.

But I didn't value it as much as I could have. We'd go out together, and I would attack the alcohol and drugs aggressively, as I usually did. Dakota wouldn't say much about that, but I knew she didn't like what I was doing. I could see it in her eyes, her half-smile that turned into a frown. She watched what I was doing, and inside it was eating her alive. I took her for granted. Dakota would join me on nights out. I learned later that she did that because she knew if she came with me, I would be less focused on my phone (as I was during the day) and more focused on the people around me, including her. It was her way of trying to get time with me.

After a few weeks, she sat me down. "You don't need any of this," she said. "You have an amazing personality and people around you who love you. You are going to hurt yourself, and more importantly, you are hurting everyone who cares about you most. I'm always worried about you. Please keep this in mind. Don't be selfish."

She's wrong. She's looking at it all wrong.

"I'm fine," I told her. It didn't matter that by this point she wasn't the only one who had said something to me about my substance abuse. My family and close friends had weighed in, too. But I knew they were all wrong. I was a master of living on the edge. Nothing could go wrong because I was invincible. I knew myself, and I knew I had this under control.

She warned me that if I didn't face my demons, if I didn't make changes in my life, she wasn't going to stay with me. We bickered about it, but she held her ground.

After only a couple of months of dating, my old-soul, vegan unicorn broke up with me because I was not willing to face my problem. Not that I saw it that way at the time. *I am right and she is wrong,* I told myself. My ego was in charge: utterly stubborn, single-minded, and selfish.

I also have a very good mouth. I couldn't let her out of my life that easily, so I convinced her that I would work on "my issues" for the sake of our relationship. I didn't need to work on myself, of course, because I was just fine. I would work on the relationship. That's what needed attention. Not me.

* * *

Father's Day falls on a Sunday in mid-June. In 2015, I knew I would make the seventy-mile drive out to Moreno Valley to see my family that day in my pearl white S550 Mercedes, as I did every couple of weeks.

I had to work the night before at Warwick. Normally Dakota would have come out to the club too, but she was too tired. She went home to her apartment and texted *"Good night babe, have a great night at work, I'll see you tomorrow to visit your family, love you."*

I was stressed out about Father's Day and how I wanted to be there for my father. So I did the exact opposite of what I should have done to have a great time with my dad. I started drinking and doing drugs. The higher I got, the more stressed out I got about the fact that I was getting high. I told myself to stop, but I couldn't.

I got home but was so high I couldn't sleep. I kept drinking. I could see I was going to be awake all night, and this was going to piss Dakota off. I was letting her down once again. That expectation just made me more stressed out.

I tried to force myself to sleep, but of course that didn't work and just stressed me out more. I lay flat on my bed with my eyes closed, wide awake. I was tired but wired. The more I tried to sleep, the more I thought about how bad it was that I couldn't sleep, the more anxiety I had about Dakota and my family, and the worse I felt.

You can't show up to see Mom and Dad like this. You can't miss Father's Day, though. That would be a huge letdown and disrespectful. Just tell them the truth.

I was ashamed of myself. So what did I do? The opposite of what that voice was telling me to do: I'd decided I'd go with the flow and figure it out.

I finally dragged myself into the shower, but I was exhausted.

Just do some blow. You can keep yourself awake on the drive.

So I did. I couldn't face Dakota, so I texted some lame excuse about not sleeping well and deciding to go earlier. She could read me like a hawk, and immediately called me out. "Did you do drugs?" she demanded, and I confessed. She was angry and said she wasn't going to come to my parents at all.

Somehow, I made the drive safely, but I wasn't fooling anybody. As soon as I walked into my parents' house, they looked into my intoxicated eyes and knew something was up. But that was okay, because in a moment of amazing stupidity I had brought more cocaine to keep myself awake while I hung out with my dad.

You've really lost your mind, Eli.

That thought might be the very first time I considered that I might have a problem. But it didn't stick.

Not that my family didn't try. Father's Day turned into an impromptu AA-style "intervention." My parents sat with me in their living room and said how much they wanted to help me. They didn't argue with me, but they wanted to know how they could help me take the first step away from the party life. While this was going on, my sister called Dakota, who made the drive from LA to join us after Diana filled her in on what was happening.

As soon as she walked in, she wrapped her arms around me and said, "I love you, Eli." Over the next few hours, though, she made it clear that if I did not get my act together, she was going to leave me for good.

"No good can come of this, son," my mother said through her tears. She described how she lived in fear of waking up to news of something tragic happening to me. "Please," she begged, "you can figure out life without this lifestyle. Leave before it's too late."

Get out of nightlife? No way. This is my life. I can't give it up.

My defense mechanisms and my powers of denial were so strong that I was able to sit in my parents' home, look my crying mother in the face, and tell myself that nightlife had no connection to my drug or alcohol problems.

As I've said, we are a reflection of the people around us. Every night I surrounded myself with like-minded individuals who drank, snorted, popped, or smoked one kind of intoxicant or another, and told themselves they didn't have a problem. If they didn't, then neither did I. I could not fathom how I could work in nightlife and not consume drugs and alcohol, and that's all I was concerned about. I was so selfish I could not see the emotional rollercoaster ride I was taking everyone around me on.

Jammed into that living room, I finally agreed I would make some changes.

Some.

I would make wiser choices, I said. I'd be careful about my partying. I would pick and choose my rages more carefully. I'd slow down.

What I could not agree to was the idea that I had to leave the nightlife world. I had so much more to accomplish, and I was not about to walk away from something I had spent five years building. I had a point to prove to all the critics, all my followers, everyone around me watching my rise and hoping for my fall. I was starting to attract attention from some people in the industry who resented my success and wanted to see me fail. The culture in Los Angeles was very much one of every man for himself. (It was different than in Miami or Las Vegas, where earnings and tips often were pooled and split among teams.)

I couldn't give them any ammunition. I had something to prove to the world, after all. I couldn't walk away and look like a quitter. I was too concerned about what *they* think.

My joy and happiness depended on what other people thought about me. I lived to smell the smoke they blew up my ass:

"Dude, you're killing it!"

"You're living the dream, brother!"

"How do I attain this lifestyle?"

"I'll do anything to walk in your shoes!"

Yes, I loved that flattery. I cared deeply about the opinions of people who, actually, I didn't care about at all. I might have met them at a club. More likely, I knew them through social media. I had no real relationship with them. Most of them I'd never even seen physically. They had no idea who I actually was, what deep issues I struggled with, or what truly mattered to me. Yet I let them and their opinions run my life. I lived for their approval.

So I told my family and Dakota that I could manage my inner demons—even though I had manifestly proved that, in fact, I could not manage them. We all bought into that delusion because I didn't give them any other choice. I was still determined to own my own club or partner with someone else who owned one. I didn't know myself well enough to understand what really mattered, or should matter. Instead, I deflected the love and concern my family and girlfriend showed me, put my head down, and vowed I would accomplish the goal I set myself when I first walked into Kress.

I am going to own a club. Stick to the vision. Stick to the plan. Onward and upward.

Mom, Dad, Sis and I

＊ ＊ ＊

Two weeks later, the universe smacked me on the side of the head.

Hard.

One of my best friends before I met Dakota was a guy named Lucas. I met a lot of people at Playhouse and Warwick, of course, but Lucas and I really clicked. He'd been a professional basketball player for eleven years, including a stint in the NBA. He was sarcastic, funny, popular, and very successful with women. We shared similar interests and personality traits. We went on vacation together to Mexico, went to comedy nights, played paintball, went to house parties—always with a ton of beautiful girls. We were like Beavis and Butthead together.

Lucas looked like a Greek god—he was in amazing shape and seemed invincible. As far as I was concerned, he had life figured out.

We hung out together a lot, growing close over the years as we partied, traveled together, and talked about our pasts and futures. We seemed to bring out the best in each other. I came to think of him as a blood brother. He was loyal to me, too. He was a regular for me at the clubs where I hosted, not only bringing his famous and wealthy friends but also sharing his contacts with me—something you never see in this greedy city.

We did a lot of things together. But mostly, we partied. Half the time we spent together was during one kind of party or another.

There is a golden rule among men: Never let a woman get in between your friendship. Yet we violated it. Back before I met Dakota, I had been dating a girl for a while, and we had just broken up when Lucas invited her and another girl over to his house. "We just split," I said to him. "Why would you invite her over? You're my best friend!"

He didn't think it mattered, but I did. "Bro, I would never do this to you," I said.

"How the hell are you going to talk to me like that?" he replied.

Our argument blew up and our friendship fell apart. If we competed over a woman today, I wouldn't be nearly as upset. I've grown a lot from the young, immature, aggressive man I was then. At the time, we both had strong personalities and egos, and I certainly didn't know how to just talk it out. So we didn't. I came at him hard emotionally, he responded, and that was that. The friendship was toast.

My pride cost me my best friend, but I couldn't see it that way at the time.

Screw it. It is what it is. Life goes on.

We continued to run into each other out on the town—nightclubs, house parties, dinners, and events. Our relationship was reduced to the occasional "What up?" as we moved past each other through the crowd. Whenever that happened, I felt upset. It was like seeing an ex-girlfriend I still cared for, wondering what could have been. Even though I wanted to say "screw it," I never stopped loving and caring for Lucas.

On June 30, 2015, I received a horrifying text message from a friend: "*Lucas was found dead in a pool.*"

I couldn't believe it. I felt like vomiting. I'd never been so thrown by something in my entire life.

No way. Not Lucas. This has to be a mistake.

It wasn't fake news. It was entirely, terribly real. He'd been partying with friends, apparently got light-headed, fell down some steps into a swimming pool when no one else was around, and drowned. That simple.

No one wanted to believe the truth. I heard people say things like, "*If it wasn't for the pool being there, he wouldn't have died. He would have just hit the floor and woke up later on.*"

Really?

After that first wave of disbelief, I didn't really feel anything. I was pretty good at denial, and I denied the meaning of Lucas's death. For a while.

Then one day Dakota and I pulled up to a Lebanese restaurant we liked. Lucas had been Lebanese, like me. Dakota ran in to grab our take-out. I sat in the car, working on a farewell social media post about Lucas. Some of what I wrote about our adventures made me laugh out loud. But the dawning realization that this was my last message about a man who had been my best friend sent tears down my cheeks.

When she returned, I was sobbing. I didn't take well to the Catholic church when I was growing up, but I am a very spiritual person. Religion doesn't work for me, but I believe in a higher power. I believe that what you do in this life, who you truly are in your heart, determines the direction of your next life. Lucas's death broke me in a way I had not been broken before. I had never lost a close friend or family member.

"I'm really sorry Eli, I really am," Dakota said as she wrapped her arms around me. "This is a terrible tragedy. My heart goes out to you and his friends. But let this be an eye-opener. I couldn't ever imagine this happening to you. Please wake up! Learn from this. Stop using drugs and quit drinking. You don't need it, for the millionth time. I love you. I care for you more than you know, and I'm always here for you."

So what did I do?

I got *lit* for Lucas's memorial. I was high on cocaine and alcohol for that solemn event. If you want to judge me, go ahead—I was in such denial, so out of control, and I was no different than those people insisting that the pool killed him, not the drugs. Or give me the benefit of the doubt, and see me as a very confused, lost soul, spiraling down into a hole of ever-deepening denial.

You cannot change someone who does not see a problem with

their behavior or question the rightness of their own actions. You cannot change someone who does not want to change themselves, for themselves. They have to change in their own time, relying on their own reasons. Some people have to go far, far down the hole until they hit rock bottom before they find those reasons.

As far as I was concerned, I was just fine. In fact, I was still on my way down.

FIVE

THE LETTER

"When you find peace within yourself, you become the kind of person who can live at peace with others."

—PEACE PILGRIM

WORK WAS FRONT-AND-CENTER OF MY LIFE EVER since I started in the nightlife world. I believed my job was to build relationships, and I worked at it ceaselessly. Days, nights, weekends, I was on my phone. That little screen was the worst of all my addictions, actually. I'm all-in on whatever I do, and now, in mid-2016, thriving at Warwick, I was all-in on social media.

First thing I did when I woke up was grab my phone and begin scrolling: Instagram, Facebook, Twitter, Snapchat. These were my daily news. I had to see what everyone was up to, and I had to put together my own posts. I'd post, then refresh and read back through again. I'd read my own posts repeatedly, something I didn't realize I was doing at the time.

They don't call these things "cell" phones for nothing. I was a prisoner of my device, consumed by messages, comments, views and likes, who was getting what kind of buzz, what other people—*they*—were thinking and doing and saying and posting and liking and dissing. My hands were handcuffed during all my waking hours to the addictive, twisted world of social media flowing through that little cell phone.

I told myself I had no choice. I had to keep up with what everyone else was doing, because I thought that was my job. It was how I stayed relevant, in the know. The "job" excuse was that—an excuse that allowed me to hide my deeply antisocial behavior in social media. I actually was suffering from nomophobia (no-mobile-phone phobia).

People around me saw my behavior for what it was. My family and friends called me on it constantly, because when I was with them, I wasn't really with them at all. I could be at an event, out for dinner with Dakota, visiting my family, hanging out with friends, but one thing was always the same: I was on the screen. "It's for work, guys," I'd say. "Relax."

We make time for what we want to make time for: friendships, romantic relationships, business. If someone wants to make time for you, they will. If they don't think you are more important than something else, they won't. I didn't think anything was more important than my constant presence on and connection to social media.

It's your money-maker, Eli. Don't listen to them.

My professional relationships—let's call them connections, because most of them weren't true relationships—continued to expand as I took care of business at Warwick. I had about 50,000 followers on social media, and 6,000 or 7,000 people in my phone's address book. Some of them were pretty solid relationships, including a friendship I developed with a guy I'll call Taylor, one of the world's best-selling music artists. He was the biggest pop star of our generation, someone who sold out the Staples Center whenever he performed in LA. He loved the nightlife, so when he hit me up on a summer evening to come to Warwick Wednesday, I knew it was going to be *on*. This guy was *famous* famous, not just internet famous.

Warwick Wednesday was our marquee night, famed around Hollywood for featuring a collection of stars and starlets no other club could compete with. Dakota joined me that night, and we all had a fantastic time.

Except...Taylor had a thing for Dakota, and he didn't make a secret of it. During Women Crush Wednesday (#WCW), on Instagram he posted on his timeline three pictures of women he had a "crush" on: I recall seeing Beyoncé, Halsey, and my girlfriend, Dakota. This went out to his huge following; I think it was nearly a hundred million followers then. It was a slap in the face—is that the sort of thing a real friend would do? But I kept my mouth shut.

His #WCW post was the kind of act that showed me the true nature of a lot of the "friends" I had in Hollywood. Because the truth was neither Dakota nor I could respond the way we really wanted to. I had to swallow my pride to keep certain relationships around for the business side of my life. We didn't respond in any way, because we didn't want to give it any energy. We played along and didn't put any emotion into it. Taylor was trying to push my buttons, but I couldn't let him.

One of the realities of the nightlife business is that pretty much everyone is trying to get something from everyone else. Being associated with Taylor was good for my brand. I didn't want to burn that up by getting jealous of his interest in my girlfriend. Instead, I told myself that he had given me kind of a cool compliment. That was the story I tried to convince myself of, but I didn't really believe it.

Another truth about Hollywood is that everyone is on the make for the next best thing. They always think the grass is greener somewhere else (even if it isn't). The next role, the next job, the next relationship, the next hook-up—that's the high everyone seeks. Taylor had a lot of success in his life, yet he envied things about my life. Especially Dakota.

As that Warwick Wednesday wound down, Dakota and I joined Taylor and his posse at Kitchen 24, an all-night diner a block from the club. Taylor wanted to have a pool party at his house the next day, so he and I huddled over who to invite and how to put the event together. As we left the diner the paparazzi swarmed our group. That was no big deal—it happened a lot when I was out with notable friends. The next day, though, a picture of Dakota next to a hoodie-wearing Taylor splashed across the gossip pages with the question, "Who's the beautiful mystery brunette spotted getting in a car at the end of the night with Taylor?"

The news media is a vile thing. Headlines are just clickbait to get attention, even though they can destroy reputations and ruin lives. Editors who cover Hollywood seem determined to filter and shape stories to fit their agenda, never mind the truth. Taylor may have liked that photo—after all, he was into Dakota—and he may have thought he could steal her from me. I've always believed that if a girl I was dating wanted to be with someone else, she should go be with that person. Dakota never made me feel that way, though. She made me feel secure, and I never doubted her love for and commitment to me. That day, plenty of other people who "knew" me might have thought that my girl and Taylor were a thing, but I knew I just had to brush it off and go on. After all, anyone who really knew us knew it was a hoax.

The pool party should have been a cool event, but it was actually the day my relationship with Taylor ended. His place was gorgeous, an enormous estate in a quiet neighborhood surrounded by a lake. As Dakota lay out by the pool, Taylor stared at her. "Man, she is something else, bro," he said. "You got the best of the best. Where can I find one like her? You're the man. She's absolutely perfect."

Don't get agitated, Eli. Yeah, it's strange that your so-called friend is staring your girl up and down, but you know what to do. Take it as a compliment.

Later that afternoon, Taylor insisted we play a game of touch football. "Let's bond! We never bond, we're just out partying all the time. Let's hang out like real friends would."

Something about this didn't feel right, but I ignored my gut. A few plays into the game, I told our team captain, who was a friend of Taylor's and a DJ, that I was going to go long—he should throw deep. I took off from the line, burned the defender, and turned around to see the ball coming over my shoulder. I made the catch, turned again, and crashed chest-first into an enormous wooden pool chair. The collision knocked me out cold.

I woke up to hear Taylor laughing. "You're lucky it wasn't an inch higher, that would have ripped your face off." I could barely breathe. Something was wrong. Several people were telling me to go to the hospital.

"He doesn't need to go to the hospital! Take a shot, some tequila will do the trick," Taylor said. I sat with Dakota, but I couldn't catch my breath and started wheezing. My hands started to freeze up. Pissed off at Taylor, Dakota loaded me into her car and took me to the hospital, where I was diagnosed with a fractured sternum. My hands had stopped working because I had gone into shock, the doctor said.

I'd had enough of Taylor. I knew that day what his intentions were and what kind of guy he was, and I didn't need that in my life.

We grew apart. I think both of us knew a line had been crossed that day. That was unusual, because I spent my nights and days cultivating relationships, not breaking them apart. A couple of years later, he apologized to me. I thought I had seen him at Coachella in 2019, and texted him. He wasn't there but shot me a text right back: "I'm sorry for being a dick at my house that day.

That's not even in my heart, hope you don't hold that over me. Please forgive me." And I did truly forgive him. People change and grow. Forgiveness is a form of peace and the ultimate form of happiness. When you forgive, you heal. When you let go, you grow.

I was thriving in Hollywood. But the relationship that should have mattered the most was in a death spiral.

Dakota and I rented a house together in late November of 2015. Now that we were together 24/7, we realized how hard living together actually is. I had lived with a woman before, I knew how challenging it could be, and I wasn't as keen on moving in as Dakota was. We got along for the most part, but then I would do something that would cause Dakota to decide we needed some time apart. When that happened I would sit down and handwrite a letter in which I tried to apologize and explain how much I loved and cared for her. I meant every word I wrote at the time I wrote them, but you can only do that so many times before your partner has had enough.

In other words, what I did mattered a lot more than what I said.

A few weeks after Taylor's pool party, Dakota and I broke up, although we continued to share our house for four more months. I was confident I could win her back because we were still physically near, but I was wrong. Her mind was made up.

I shouldn't have been surprised when it was my turn to find a letter from her. She had continued to live with me, she wrote, because she still loved me.

When we first met you said I fell for your lifestyle, the way you lived. I need you to know that isn't true, no matter what your friends say or make you believe from here on out.... I truly believe that if we met under different circumstances and we weren't in this industry, we could have made it. I saw myself sitting in the backyard drinking tea, watching birds fly when we were older. I couldn't wait to spend the rest of my life with you and grow old together, but I feel like no matter what job we have in life, if it was meant to be, the person would understand so much that it could never come between them. So, maybe we aren't meant to be.

My partying, she said, hurt her heart. The endless conflict between us was rooted in the fact that I didn't accept her point of view that I had any kind of problem—a substance abuse problem, an attention problem, a phone addiction. "I wish you could see life through my eyes sometimes," she wrote. "I think you'd feel my pain and would really understand, but this can never happen."

The whole letter broke my heart. Perhaps the hardest part to read was when she described how I had made her lose confidence in herself.

You can entertain yourself with your phone, memes, videos, group chats, sports all day. That's just you. To get your attention, what I'm saying has to be more engaging than what you're already tuned into. I used to have so much confidence before you, now I struggle to think that in order to be heard, I have to be worthwhile, because we aren't into the same things in life, we've driven a wedge between ourselves. In order to spend time, I've had to coax it out of you. It shouldn't be this way on either side, because you want to be the best at your job, you've eliminated the possibility of me in your life. Unless I fit into the schedule or participate,

I can't see you or spend quality time, to you, sitting on a couch sharing memes is bonding, but I would like something much deeper. Something you have, but it doesn't fit in to the way you run your life. It hurts to suppress myself in order not to weird you out or push you away. It hurts to look at someone in the eye explaining your heart out and they can't comprehend your feelings. I don't think you're a bad person. I don't think you've intentionally done things. I just know that I deserve to be understood and not explain myself over careless actions....

I've figured out why I always wanted to go to Disneyland, Six Flags, etc. It was because they were places that had attractions that would take your attention away from the social media/work world. I hoped this would take you away from the life you're so caught up on, and you'd be able to live with me in that moment....

As I sit beside you, drive in the passenger seat next to you, sit at the chair across from you at lunch, you barely look at me. So when you're at your job, all of this dies down because everyone you're watching on social media is there. You actually semi are living in the moment. This is why I engage in your work. I'd rather sit beside you at the club, go to events with you, on occasion party with you. This is all done in hopes of receiving your attention. This is all done in the hopes that I can be acknowledged and get to see Eli without distractions.

Then, because we don't see eye to eye, in that short span of time, if I am upset by you doing something, you tell me I can never be happy, I ruin your work, we live together there's no need to be together all of the time, I'm being crazy. It's as if sitting at home beside you, sitting in the car next you, sleeping in the same bed as you, sitting across from you at lunch and keeping my feelings to myself would be the way I should live.

I tried it for a while. It's more hurtful than anything I've experienced. I just want you to know that I am different than anyone else you will meet because, I love you.

Denial is a powerful thing. Even as I read these words, I felt that Dakota simply didn't understand me, when it was evident that she understood me all too well. I was blind to what really mattered. We were communicating, but we weren't comprehending—at least I wasn't. Communication without comprehension is just noise, and I was not willing or able to comprehend what Dakota had been telling me about myself for a year and a half.

Dakota was more right than ever, but even after I cried over that letter—something I still do every time I read it—I couldn't comprehend why she felt the way she did. My little vegan queen, my best friend, my lover, was gone from my life. I had hurt her enormously, undercutting her confidence without ever meaning to.

My heart ached.

She's right. I need to work on myself once again. But what do I work on if I don't see a problem with my actions? She just doesn't understand my lifestyle. She never will.

Like I said, denial is a real son of a bitch.

SIX

HIGH TIDES, DARK TIMES

"Sometimes we go back and repeat an old mistake just so that we can remember why we moved forward."

—YUNG PUEBLO

THREE, TWO, ONE, HAPPY NEW YEAR! I CELEBRATED December 31, 2016, with a warm midnight kiss with Dakota at Warwick. Then we rushed home to throw a few more items in our suitcases. Early morning found us westbound out of LAX on the first flight of the day to Oahu.

Despite the conviction in Dakota's letter, I had won her back again. We saw each other at a MAXIM party, locked eyes, and soon (with the help of friends urging us on), I had talked my way back into her life. By now I was repeating myself in our relationship. I told her I'd clean up my act (for the relationship—never for myself). I knew that's what she wanted. She didn't demand it, but it was clear that either I would get clean or she would leave.

Part of my problem was that I kept taking her for granted. I told myself it didn't really matter what I did. She would tolerate my partying, my endless focus on my business and my phone, the way I was with her without actually being present for her. That's how I'd acted, partly because I felt I always could get her back. I'd done it so many times! Even though she was incredibly special to me, I behaved like I didn't care that much.

Now, I promised her I'd change. So we tried again.

And I did change. I got clean and sober. I actually enjoyed it. But a little voice in the back of my head said, "If she leaves again, you know you are diving right back in."

For two years Dakota had been begging me to travel with her, but I was always caught up in my work, too worried that I'd miss out on something, too afraid to leave Hollywood for even a moment and perhaps jeopardize my relevancy or my connections. When we stepped off the Virgin Atlantic flight to the words, "Aloha, welcome to Hawaii," and the smell and feel of a lei of frangipani flowers being placed around our necks, that was a dream come true for Dakota.

I had made the trip a surprise, telling her only a few days before we left. Her birthday and our anniversary coincided with the start of the year, so we had a triple celebration. She was my ride-or-die—I owed her this. We had experienced two years of love, laughter, tears, and the best friendship I could ask for. I felt blessed to have her by my side.

It felt so good to be away from the noise and chaos of our lives in Los Angeles, reveling in the clear tropical air of an ocean-view resort at Waikiki. The next day we rented a jeep and drove north, blasting old-school Sugar Ray, Sublime, and 311 out the open windows, waving our hands in the warm air. We joined some friends, professional surfers on the North Shore who were living in a beachside home provided by their sponsors. It was amazing to watch the sunset there with the love of my life wrapped in my arms.

I stayed off social media except for making a few posts. I promised Dakota I would be more present for her during the trip, and I was. I posted so people could see what we were doing, but I didn't get caught up in the endless scroll. I wanted to share our authentic love—not brag about it, but show it for what it is. Plenty of people knew we were together. I wanted to show how great "together" actually was, and she tolerated my doing that.

The trip was everything a vacation should be. It reminded me of the Vince Vaughn/Jason Bateman film *Couples Retreat*, only without all the drama. We swam with sharks and sea turtles, worked out daily, had romantic dinners in the soft tropical air, enjoyed couples' massages. The whole thing was magical.

And then we went back to reality.

Within a month, Dakota and I had split up again. I dove deep into the nightlight circus and social media, and she wouldn't tolerate it. Yes, I was still sober, but I wasn't able to find balance with her. She wasn't the priority I should have made her. Dakota kept me grounded and helped me see what mattered in life, but I couldn't seem to stick to that wisdom. As I went through my days without her, my heart ached.

What's a king without his queen?

Although we texted occasionally, we kept it short. She was growing numb to my bullshit and behavior, even as I was deep in pain over losing her.

I couldn't seem to change, to find in myself the me that she said she loved, and to keep that version of myself front and center.

I had been Dakota's first romantic partner when she got to LA. She was still young, she was a very hot model, and I knew she wanted, even needed, to learn some lessons about this twisted, sick city on her own.

As for me, well, my birthday was coming up, and that was going to be a bigger party than ever. I was born on April 14, but I celebrated it on April 12—the night before the Coachella Valley Music and Arts Festival. That is one of the largest, most famous and most profitable music festivals in the world. I wouldn't miss it for anything, nor would any of the other elite party-goers who were my business and my world.

Every year I stressed out about the party I put together for myself.

I made sure to schedule it for that opening night because that meant I could get everyone I wanted there. Most of the taste-makers, stars, and starlets from all over whom I wanted to stay connected with would be at Coachella, which meant they could be at my party.

This year was going to be an especially huge celebration because I had finally achieved the milestone I had been driving toward for years—and it had been announced on a giant billboard on Santa Monica Boulevard. In early April a huge new sign went up above the landmark Santa Palm carwash:

WARWICK

Coming Summer 2017

#WarwickNo8 #WelcomeToParadise

XOXO—T.R., Jacques, & Eli

At last, I was a partner in a nightclub, and the whole city knew it. I actually hadn't known the billboard was coming. After years of loyalty, a day-one-level grind, and a consistent willingness to swallow my pride in the pursuit of my goal, Warwick's partners and I had hammered out a deal for me to be a partner in the eighth remodel of Warwick. (We started remodeling once or twice a year—people loved it, no other club was doing it, and it drove business through the roof.)

In early April, Jacques called and said, "Go drive down Santa

Monica Boulevard. When you see the car wash, look up. You're with us now, Eli. Welcome to the top!"

Of course I took the drive right away, and the effect was stunning. My name was literally in lights over West Hollywood, and my phone was lighting up with calls and texts from friends all over Hollywood. They were happy for me, and I was happy for me. I felt victorious. Not only was Warwick marketing its eighth makeover, but it was also marketing me to the entire city of Los Angeles.

I had *arrived*.

I had promised myself eight years earlier that I was going to own or be a partner in a nightclub, and I had done it.

My name is up there. Thank you to all the haters, doubters and shit-talkers, all the bored people who hate their own lives and take pleasure in talking trash on social media about someone trying to make something from nothing. I wouldn't have gotten this far without you.

Yeah, I had a personality. I could hold a hard line with people as I made sure nobody walked on me. Maybe I came across as cocky. Maybe I should have been a little humbler. But if I had, maybe my name wouldn't be on that billboard.

As I said, Coachella, one of the biggest events of the year, was coming up. So was my birthday. I had a lot to celebrate.

I had set myself up to be the guy to throw the best event the night before the festival—my birthday party—when everyone could come. Of course, this conflicted directly with my desire to stay sober. I had been clean and sober for six months. People had come out for me. I knew that a lot of these people were degenerates who planned to destroy their bodies and get shitfaced for the next four days straight, functioning on as little sleep as possible to enjoy every second they could.

It's your birthday, Eli. Enjoy it. You can party. People are coming to celebrate you tonight. Booze it up. Live it up!

I always made sure my birthday party offered everything anyone could want, and this night was no different. I normally hosted in a private room at a restaurant I liked. There was tons of food and plenty of booze. Without Dakota in my life, I drank that night, and after six months of being sober, it felt like a relief.

This event was work—I curated a careful list of a couple dozen friends who were also celebrities and influencers, and after dinner made sure we all went to Warwick, sold it out, and had an epic night. My birthday nights were special: the club always hit max capacity extremely early, and crowds of people would be stuck outside with no way of getting in.

Over the years, surprise live performances and special guest appearances happened organically. Notable faces like The Chainsmokers, Halsey, Paris Hilton, Odell Beckham Jr., Logan Paul, Nicole Scherzinger, and others would pop up. I never knew who it might be until the last moment because it depended on who was in town and actually showed after they confirmed they would be attending. I didn't pay for any of this—their decision to show face was just based on my personal relationships with each of them.

In 2019, Machine Gun Kelly, G-Eazy, and Ty Dolla $ign jumped on the microphone, performed a hit or two on stage, and hyped up the crowd:

"Fuck with Eli, get some money!"

"Marathon Godz!"

"We need eight cases of water for Eli tonight!"

Between Machine Gun Kelly and G-Eazy on the mic, they had the laughs rolling and the energy going off. I was completely wasted and shattered but enjoying the moment as best I could.

I should have felt on top of the world the next day when I boarded the high-end party bus a friend had chartered for the run east on Interstate 10 to Coachella, which is near Palm Springs. There was plenty of booze, beautiful women, and a lot of friends.

"Happy birthday to you, happy birthday to you, happy birthday dear Eliiiii, happy birthday to you!"

They all sang for me. But I wasn't feeling it. I had achieved my dream of being a partner in a nightclub, but I felt empty. I told myself I shouldn't—after all, this is what I had worked for. I always have been hard on myself, telling myself to work harder, do more. Now I was on top, and I felt emptier than ever.

As far as the people around me were concerned, I was crushing it. Yet I had lost the person I loved most, which sent me into a deep depression I couldn't share with anyone. So I began to put up a façade of happiness that would become all too familiar to me: the fake smile, the appearance of having a good time. I called it The Mask.

On that birthday bus, I thanked each person who sang for me. But the person I most wanted to be with me wasn't there. Dakota had flipped a switch for me. She tried to show me what mattered and what didn't in life. She wanted me to value and prioritize different things than the shallow people around me and what they did or thought. She got me to see that I didn't really care about all my so-called "friends" in LA nightlife, and they didn't really care about me.

How can I feel so empty inside? I worked so hard to get here. My Day-One dreams have come true, and this is just the beginning. Snap out of it, Eli.

I knew I was going to run into Dakota at the festival, because everybody who is anybody is there, and I wasn't looking forward to it. In fact, the prospect stressed me out.

It all came together—the relief and success of achieving my dream with Warwick, the achievement of a half-year sober, the pressure of making sure my friends had an amazing event, the excitement of the Coachella festival, and my anguish over losing Dakota and worrying that I was going to run into her. The result: another deep dive into the dark, too familiar hole of drugs and alcohol.

If you looked at my life from the outside, as most of the public who followed me did, you'd probably tell yourself that I was living the life everyone aspired to. How could I have any problems? How could anything really be wrong? I worked hard to maintain that image, curating the company of beautiful women, nice cars, excellent clothing, expensive watches. I smiled and laughed, was witty and entertaining. And I really do love being entertaining—I love seeing those around me enjoying themselves.

What they couldn't see, and what the larger public couldn't even suspect, was that inside I was rotting, depressed, and running away from my inner demons. Partying was an excellent way to mask who I was and what was going on with me.

Mask on.

And so I celebrated six months of sobriety with an epic bender.

Am I an idiot?

Those people I was calling degenerates, the ones who would party for four straight days, running on booze and drugs and no sleep? Yeah, that was me. They were, when I think back on it, people I really didn't know at all, even though the drugs made me believe we were "family." When I finally understood that, I thought, "What a coke head."

What did I get for that epic bender that weekend? Sure enough, I ran into Dakota when I was high out of my mind. I was sitting on a bench with some friends. I had been drinking and had just taken a dose of MDMA (also called Ecstasy) when I saw her walk by holding hands with another guy.

MDMA really puts you in your feelings and emotions. Well, my emotions around Dakota were already at a fever pitch, and now this. It was wrong on every level.

Already with another guy? What the hell? It's only been two months. It has to be a façade.

I damn well was going to say something to her, never mind that I didn't think there was anything wrong with me visibly frolicking around the festival with other women. The way I saw it, Dakota was embarrassing me in front of friends and colleagues. We had been known for two years as a power couple in this world. Now here she was dissing me—because, of course, everything was about me, wasn't it?

I grabbed my friend Jeff Wittek, who was also a comedian and YouTube star, to give me a little backup in case things went sideways with this new guy and marched after Dakota. I confronted them aggressively, demanding to speak with her.

"What for? And about what?" she shot back. She wasn't having any of it, and didn't want to hear anything I had to say. But my ability to talk fast and convincingly is one of my great skills, and it works even when I'm blitzed out of my head. Jeff told me later I basically quoted some of the rapper Drake's lyrics as if they were my own words. I didn't realize that at the time. I was just pouring words out at her, trying to get her to see that she was embarrassing me, making me look like a buffoon in front of my world, as if I owned the entire festival. I had no game plan for this conversation, I was just pouring out my feelings.

And then something spectacular happened. I saw a look in her eye that I read to mean, "I love you, Eli, and I'm still in love with you." At least that's what I believed she was telling me with her eyes, and that was enough for the moment.

I was still deep in emotional turmoil, but that gave me a sliver of hope that there might still be something between us, and I might still be able to get her back. I had work to do, work on myself, but there was still something there between me and her.

A week after Coachella ended, I invited Dakota over to my house— actually *our* stylish house, for I had stayed after she moved out. I kept hoping she would return someday. I wanted to speak face-to-face with her. Maybe I wanted to see if what I had read in her eyes was real? Maybe I wanted closure? Maybe I wanted to see her again in person?

In fact, I knew exactly what I wanted. She agreed to come over. I blasted the Grammy Award-winning Jackson Five classic hit "I Want You Back" through the surround-sound speakers. When she knocked on what I still thought of as *our* door, I jetted down the steps, threw the door open, wrapped my arms around her, and sang along.

She smiled and we danced around *our* home until the song was over. It was a beautiful moment. I had butterflies in my stomach, and I know she did, too. She was giggling.

We talked for hours. I explained how well work was going. Yes, I was a partner now at Warwick, and we had put together a powerful arrangement with Tao Group, a leading international hospitality and nightlife group that was new in the LA market but had huge pull. We were a mom-and-pop company but were deeply rooted in Hollywood. We and Tao definitely could help each other out. On nights when Warwick was closed, we hosted our best clients at one of their spectacular restaurants, Tao or Beauty & Essex, then moved over to either Avenue or The Highlight Room, gorgeous nightclubs they recently had opened.

This alliance kept us relevant, hip and crisp, and allowed us to benefit from their connections. They would send their bottle waitresses and staff to fill our tables, or send their clients over. On nights when Warwick was closed, I and others would host at Tao, bringing our clients over. Our collaboration was one of the most sharp-witted plays in Hollywood.

I'd also pulled together a collaboration between Dreamworks Animation, recently acquired by Universal Pictures, and the clothing brand STAMPD. I knew key players on both sides, and saw an opportunity to link them up over the release of *The Mummy*, a Tom Cruise film that Universal was releasing in June. STAMPD had rugged designs that fit the movie's aesthetic perfectly. I saw it could be a great collaboration, so I pulled together the meetings that made it happen.

The event was a party at STAMPD's South La Brea flagship store, which was transformed into a showcase of *The Mummy* props and artifacts. Guests from fashion, film, music, sports, and design came to see the unveiling of a nine-piece capsule collection of clothing designed just for the event. Everyone was excited about the event's success, but no one was more excited than me. In making this collaboration happen, I was showing myself and everyone else that my opportunities in LA were endless.

I told Dakota all this. I also told her that I was empty without her. "What good is any of this," I asked, "if I can't share it with the one I love most?"

It was an emotional moment, and it brought her to tears. Looking back, I wish we had ended the conversation there. Instead, we went out for a bite to eat. While we were both sitting outside Sun Café, one of our favorite vegan spots, she opened a can of worms.

"What have you been doing since we broke up?" she asked. "Who have you been seeing?"

Some people say I am too honest in my life. They say that sometimes it's better if "they" don't know too much. I don't agree. Especially when I'm dealing with someone I love, I'm very straightforward. I can live with being honest, even blunt. I don't want to look over my shoulder for the rest of my life because I've lied. I lay all my cards on the table and know I will sleep peacefully because I do. People may not like what they hear from me, but I believe they will respect me in the long run.

Well, Dakota did not like it at all when I told her who I had been hooking up with. I had thought that we could be honest and move on, but she was in shock. Whereas I had been hanging out with other women, she had resolved to stay single when we broke up, and that's what she had done. She didn't yet know who she was or where she was going, and she needed to figure that out on her own. She needed time alone so she could connect with who she really was, not with who someone was telling her she was. She needed to find out what inspired her and figure out how she wanted to grow and where she wanted to put her energy.

She might respect me for being honest someday, but right then she was upset with me, and she certainly wasn't going to come back into my life as my lover and my queen. So I went on without her.

I continued to wear my mask, smiling and wisecracking while I rotted inside. I partied hard. I hooked up with women, but that only made me feel worse.

Toward the end of June, Dakota and I started to hang out a little bit. We ended up spending a beautiful night together on July 3, and then headed to Malibu. Each of us had made separate plans there, but we promised we'd connect that night.

I didn't hear from her during the day. Immediately I thought the worst.

Is she with another guy, or is she falling for me again? Is she running away from her emotions or fighting them off? What is happening?

In my fear and insecurity, I went on a cocaine-and-alcohol-fueled bender, blowing up her phone with texts and voice messages. I couldn't control myself. I felt I was losing my mind. Late that night, she responded. She didn't really explain why she had been missing in action, but I knew from a mutual friend that by now she understood how our cycle was going to go down, and she didn't want to deal with it again.

I also knew I had blown it—this time for good. Yes, she was still worried about me, still worried about the addiction spiral I was descending into. But I was going to go on that trip alone.

She thinks I'm a nut case. No fixing this now. No way we are getting back together. I've ruined it for good. Mask on again, and off we go.

A TRIP DOWN
MEMORY LANE

SEVEN

LIFE & DEATH

"Accountability breeds response-ability."

—STEPHEN R. COVEY

MOVING ON WITH MY LIFE, OR TRYING TO, MEANT putting Dakota out of my head. I began hanging out with a young Canadian model named Brittany, a girl with brown hair and beautiful green eyes. We were friends with benefits, and in the summer of 2017, we were spending more and more time together.

I was hanging out with other girls, too, including a blond bombshell with a Playboy-level body named Amber. She had been through a breakup, too, and in late June and July, we hung together a fair bit, talking about life and our ups and downs. I felt we were really getting to know each other. Most nights I went out, Amber came with me. We seemed to be on the same wavelength, had the same commitment to partying, and liked hanging out together. There were no strings. It just felt comfortable.

Both women joined me at The Highlight Room on July 20, a Thursday, for what I expected would be another evening of hosting for Tao Group and doing what I do best—making sure people had a good time.

I remember that date because the next twenty-four hours would change my life.

The Highlight Room took up the entire top floor of Hollywood's Dream Hotel, a Tao Group property. It sprawled across 11,000 square feet and included a swimming pool that magically transformed into a dance floor beneath the stars. The night went as these nights normally did—ordinary for me, but still an epic experience of beautiful models, athletes, and A-list stars. I had my mask on, but I wasn't feeling the vibe. I kept thinking about Dakota.

At one point I even accosted a mutual girlfriend of Dakota's and mine on the dance floor, shouting over the house music about how she had avoided me in Malibu on July 4. I was on a little MDMA and very much in my feelings.

Pull it together, Eli. You are living every man's so-called dream. Why are you still stressing about her?

As the night wound down, I needed to get out of there. Wearing the mask was tiring. Nobody around me understood the emotional turmoil that consumed me. I wanted to be alone. Because I'd had a sprinkle of MDMA, a friend gave me a lift home.

Well, you're already high. What now? Invite a girl over? Continue the party and mask your emotions?

I texted Brittany. No surprise, she was pissed off that I had disappeared. But I smoothed things over. Soon she was on her way over to join me. I tried to get Amber to come over, too, but she said she was going to an after-party with some other girlfriends.

In the early morning hours, I was in touch with a guy I knew named Joey, who came over to my house. Joey always wanted to be wherever the party was. He could always get someone what they wanted when they wanted it, if you know what I mean. Brittany came over, and I was focused on kicking it with her and really didn't want anyone else around. Joey got Amber on the phone. She and a group of girls wanted to come over and hang out.

"Come on, man," he said to me, covering the phone with his hand. "Just let them come over. You don't have to hang out with them, but they want to hang out. I will make sure everyone is good, I won't mess your place up." Brittany was cool with it, and everyone was either drunk or high. I didn't want anyone to be upset.

"Fine, you can hang with them," I said. "I'll be doing my own thing."

Why am I letting all these people into my home? Just let it be, Eli. What's the worst that could happen?

At 4 a.m., Amber and her three friends showed up at my house. I really didn't want them there, but I had invited Amber earlier in the evening anyway, and if nothing else I am always a host. I spent some time in the kitchen saying hello to Amber's friends, including a brunette bombshell named Sky, with whom I exchanged social media contact information.

For the majority of the next two hours, I was in and out of my room and the living room, hanging with Brittany and checking on everyone else. I didn't feel comfortable because I didn't know everyone who was in my house, but I was not going to straight-up throw them out. Around 6 a.m. I got a text from my old friend Noah. We had grown up together in the same town, and he guessed I'd still be up partying. He wanted to come over, too, and said he'd bring some juice for mixers, as I was running low.

I sent him a screenshot of Brittany, saying I had hooked up with her. I started talking trash to him on my phone as I watched Joey try to hit on a girl named Lauren, who I had never met until that morning, on my living room chair who was falling asleep. I started jokingly trash-talking to him on my phone.

Me: Only one is weak putting her to sleep tho

Me: Coke dealer can bang her

Me: He gets the scum

Noah: On my way. By myself

Noah: Will grab chasers n*gga

Me: Ok

Me: I'm kicking 2 out to make it easier

Me: So it's just 3 all together

Noah: More the merrier fam

I know—who talks like that? My language was disgusting and disrespectful that morning—I own that, I'm not proud of it, and I'm sorry for it. For starters, let's be clear: I would never drug anybody. What I meant was, "I'm throwing everyone out of my house." You may not like it, but that's how some people talk. It wasn't out of the ordinary in my world. I'm not saying it's okay. I don't support it. But it's what we said. The truth is, what you read there was two boozed-up guys talking shit.

As soon as Noah was on his way, at 6:15 a.m., I texted Amber.

Me: U and your girl [Sky] stay with Brittany and I. I just want the other 2 gone and they leaving.

Amber: I'm on my period love. For real this time lol. Or I would be down I love Brittany.

Me: Nah just hang out. We don't gotta do that lol.

Amber: K

Me: Act like you calling an uber too so it's just us 3.

Me: It's working

Amber: Lol they left it's all good now my gf is going to stay at my place. We can go when ever

Me: U guys are good

After Joey and the other two girls left, I told Amber, Brittany, and Sky that Noah was coming by with mixers. "I just want to be around people I'm comfortable with," I said. At 7:15 a.m., I got a text from Joey thanking me for the hospitality and noting that he was headed to the house of a former professional football player we knew named Hudson. I didn't respond.

I popped out of my room to pour myself a drink, and I could feel the vibe was getting weird. Amber was getting jealous about me hanging out in private with Brittany.

God, all these people in my house! Just tell her it's time to wrap it up, it's almost 8 a.m. These are zombie apocalypse hours.

I didn't have it in me to be straightforward. I liked her a lot, and I didn't want to throw her out.

Then, Hudson, the ball player, texted to ask if he could come over to my place. Once again, somebody was hitting me up last-minute. I found out later that Amber and Hudson had already been texting.

He'd clearly been up all night and was not interested in slowing down. Like the rest of the degenerates, he had the *can't-stop-won't-stop-no-slowing-down-I'm-invincible* mentality. I didn't want to come across as rude and kick everyone but Brittany out, but I figured if Hudson came over and they all still wanted to party, maybe they'd go hang out somewhere else.

I walked out to the living room and asked Amber if it was cool to connect her to Hudson. Sure, she said, not letting me know that she and Hudson had already been texting and that she already wanted him to come over. Amber had no interest in ending the party anytime soon. Nor did Sky. *Rage, rage, rage!* This was not their first bender, that was for sure. I texted Hudson.

Me: She's getting jealous

Hudson: What's your address

Me: Of me and Brittany

Me: Nah just get Joey to get them to go to u guys

Hudson: It's just me

Hudson: He left

Me: Where R u exactly

Hudson: 20 min from your crib

Me: Do you know amber

Me: Way too far bro

Hudson: Yea I do

Me: I need them out asap

Me: Text her

Me: Hold on

Me: Gonna give u her number

Hudson: Aight

Me: [Amber's phone number]

Hudson: Ill get a hotel and I can take her there if she's down

Hudson: If she's not I can chill here idc

Hudson: Not in the mood for games

I retreated to my room to hang with Brittany. After about twenty minutes I heard Hudson join Amber, Noah, and Sky. I was playing house music in my room, and in between songs I kept hearing chit-chat in the kitchen.

Why in the hell weren't they leaving? Why haven't they gone somewhere else to party?

Between 9:17 and 9:23 a.m., Amber texted me this string of messages:

Amber: Ya good

Amber: But Your friend just poor'd half G in my drink

Amber: And I have never

Amber: Don't go to sleep come Check on mr llllllllllllqlqllqlllll

Amber: Me when you can

What the hell was she talking about?

I jumped up and went out into the kitchen. Everyone was in there talking, smiling, and looked perfectly chill.

"Are you okay?" I asked Amber.

Yeah, she said, she was fine. From what I could see, she just wanted my attention. Well, she had it. A short while later, I could see they were getting ready to leave, so I walked them all out my front door, at last. People were drunk and high, but nobody was getting dragged out or thrown over a shoulder to leave my door. They looked the way people typically looked when they left a nightclub at the end of a night.

At 3:10 that afternoon, I got a direct message from Sky on Instagram. We had just met—that was the only way she knew how to contact me.

"911! call me! Amber's not breathing!"

I called immediately. "What happened? Why did you message me? Why wouldn't you just call the police? Where is Hudson? Call the police!"

This can't be true. No way! I've seen this girl party and she can party hard. She has to be fine. Hopefully she's okay and this is just a misunderstanding.

A few hours later, I got the word that Amber was dead, apparently of a drug overdose.

I wanted to know what happened, so I reached out to Hudson. The four had left my house and gone to Sky's. Eventually Noah left. Hudson and Sky told me, when I asked them, that they had found her on the couch, her lips blue, not breathing. From my experience of hanging out with Amber for the last month, she loved booze and drugs, loved to rage, and I had seen that she carried a bottle of prescription Xanax in her purse. That, I knew, was dangerous. Mixing a drug like that with alcohol could be scary, even fatal.

I was just getting to know Amber. She was a beautiful soul, and I am deeply saddened by the situation. Yet I wasn't allowed to attend her funeral. Brittany told me that her ex-boyfriend was the one arranging the event, and he told her I shouldn't attend.

What had happened in the five-plus hours between when she left my house and when they found her on the couch?

I wish I had those answers, but I don't. Who knows what she did by herself? I felt terrible for her family and friends, but I know that as adults we all make our own decisions. She was a thirty-year-old woman who enjoyed living on the edge, like all of us did. She wanted to rage through the zombie apocalypse hours—nobody forced her to do anything, as far as I know. She had initiated contact with Hudson herself and had walked out of my house to go with him and her friends. I hadn't wanted all those people in my house in the first place that night, but once they were I made sure everyone was okay, right through when I saw them out the door.

Months later I would learn that the autopsy report showed Amber had alcohol, cocaine, and GHB (gamma-hydroxybutyrate, commonly known as the "club drug" or "date rape drug") in her blood. I wasn't there for the last few hours of her life, but I do believe she died of an accidental drug overdose. When you choose to live in the fast lane, you risk the potential consequences. Sometimes, those are lethal.

Amber's death hit me very hard. I know I will be affected by her death for the rest of my life. What happened to her could have happened to any of us. The hard, cold truth is that any of us who go hard in the paint when we party feel invincible—but we're not. *Nope! Not me! I'm superman! I'm different! I'll be fine! Let's keep lighting it up!* That mentality is not reality, and it leads to you hurting yourself or others.

Amber was another one gone too soon from heavy drug use. I really need to get my life straightened out, I thought. This could have happened to me.

Did I straighten my life out?

No.

I had a few more party nights that really flipped the switch for me, including one night when I did heavy drugs and fell over in my own house. I thought I might overdose or hurt myself. I began to worry about my health and something bad happening to me. I was no longer feeling quite so invincible.

I was working at The Highlight Room one evening the next month when I got a text from Dakota. She and I had been in occasional contact, just enough to keep me alternating between depression and hoping that I might get her back. This time, though, she said she was "severely sick" with a bad virus or the flu and wanted someone to know.

I bailed out on the party and jetted over to her house. I watched over her until she felt better and fell asleep.

That incident brought us close. We began talking about getting back together. I can't keep doing this on-again, off-again, I told her. I knew that my partying had a lot to do with our breakups. I was ready, I said, to clean up my act, go clean and sober if we got together. Yet, even as I said that I knew I was saying it for the wrong reasons. I would clean up for the relationship. Not for myself. I was going clean so we could work things out, which would just repeat our cycle of pain.

Would I ever change? Will I ever feel like I want to be completely sober, for me? Is that day ever coming?

I had a couple of friends who had gone clean and stayed clean after being degenerates like me. When you're ready to turn your life around, they told me, you'll know. Well, I wasn't feeling it yet.

Would it just be a magical feeling? Or would it take something more?

I know now that to truly love myself enough to turn my life around, I had to change my entire perspective on life. I had to shift my mindset. Effort and attitude would determine my ability to deal with the challenges I faced.

I would have to learn that mindset is everything.

EIGHT

HIGHEST HIGHS, LOWEST LOWS

"Life has officially taught me that anyone can switch up on you, no matter the history or bond you have with that person."

—ANONYMOUS

DAKOTA AND I WERE BACK ON AGAIN, AND I WAS living clean. We took a weekend in late September at a beautiful resort in Laguna Beach, and as I did when we went to Hawaii, I minimized my time on my "cell" phone. My "job" that weekend was not going to be my job—it was going to be to make her my number-one priority.

I was getting noticed by the city's media, which I really appreciated. One article in particular sent me over the moon. The day after Dakota and I got back together, I had a photo shoot with

Locale magazine at Warwick that ended up as a two-page spread. *Locale* is a taste-maker publication about the Southern California lifestyle. When I opened the magazine, I felt like a five-year-old kid who had finally gotten the present he wanted so very, very much. Being seen and recognized this way was a lifelong dream come true. The story began:

Eli Wehbe

Credentials: Partner at Warwick

Eli Wehbe is a well-versed nightclub entrepreneur and has now taken on the role of partner for Warwick. A special and sincere sense of hospitality and unique club atmosphere are what Eli and his partners have created at Warwick, and clearly his passions have paid off. He's the perfect example of taking your natural gifts and using them to create a career path that you love.

Holding a physical copy of a magazine with my picture in it, and that description of me, along with additional questions and answers that filled out the article, was surreal. The article pumped me up and inspired me. I wanted to do more than keep climbing for myself—I wanted to inspire others to pursue their paths, too. I was starting to feel I wanted to share my story, particularly my business ethic of focusing on what I want to do, ignoring critics, sticking to my vision, and grinding it out. Dakota was always telling me, "You've made all these connections with celebrities to do something bigger, to have a greater purpose." I was coming to realize that what makes my heart feel warm, what feels rewarding at the end of the day, is helping others to change their lives in a positive and meaningful way.

I got some other good press around the same time I had Dakota back in my life, and Warwick was doing great. I was thriving. Life was good.

Except for one thing.

I knew a guy named Alex who liked to play Inspector Gadget and piece together whatever irresponsible content he could in order to attract attention on social media. His main objective seemed to be to bash people in the limelight, and that included me. He started pushing a fake narrative about me on his gossip site that I'll call TheGrime. This was extremely toxic, driven by Alex's interest in bullying and harassment. Someone could take a photo, make up a story, send it in, and if Alex thought it was going to attract attention, he'd put it up. Anyone who wanted to then could comment anonymously or under a fake name, and the comments were often vicious. He loved seeing people tormenting each other because of misleading news and fake information that anyone could send in anonymously.

You have to be a sick and twisted person to decide this is how you are going to make a living, but that's what Alex did. But Amber's death looked like money to him—any juicy gossip about what might have happened was sure to drive viewers to his site, and more viewers meant more eyeballs, which meant more adver-tising revenue. In a situation like that, Alex was going to post, and keep posting, regardless of whether he might ruin my life or someone else's.

As far as I was concerned, Alex and I got along. I knew him, and we had no obvious problems. But I knew he couldn't be trusted. I knew he loved to put something up and watch the comments pile up as anonymous people said the worst possible things. In my opinion, it was pretty clear that he sometimes impersonated people and posted as them in order to stoke the conflict and outrage. Anything to make the pot boil, he did it. The more action, the more traction, the more money. It was a sad and disgusting way to live.

While Dakota and I were trying to relax in Laguna Beach, Alex was posting about me, trying to tie me into his twisted theories about what happened on the morning before Amber's death. He wouldn't talk directly to me—although he certainly could have. He behaved as if he was doing me a favor—he would post negative things about me, and then passive-aggressively pretend to defend me. He was facilitating a toxic stew on his site. He tried everything he could to get my attention and get me to engage on the site, because he knew that would blow his viewership up even bigger.

I wouldn't be baited. Just as I didn't give Taylor any of my energy when he was hitting on Dakota, I wasn't going to give Alex's bullshit any energy, either. The best thing to do in situations like this is to not respond. A response is what Alex and people like him want, because that keeps their "story" alive and moving. It fuels the fire.

So he or someone else decided to impersonate me. A comment appeared on TheGrime with my name attached to it:

Eli Wehbe

She died of an OD. End of story. She chose to take her life.

Move on!

Ps Warwick will be going off tonight. Everyone come out and celebrate Amber's life. That's what she would have wanted.

The next day, another comment:

Eli Wehbe

And if you must know Warwick had record numbers last night.

No one with any common decency would ever write anything like those comments after someone passed away. Beyond that, why would I write something idiotic about Warwick and publicize it? Anyone who thought about these comments for a moment, and who knew anything about me, knew they weren't coming from me. But of course, lots of people who followed this so-called scandal did not know me, and they drew different conclusions.

Eventually, the criticism died down. My life went on. Then, in late December of 2017, a guy I knew named Brad, who was a modern-day Hugh Hefner and a pretty good athlete, among his other attributes, shot me a message with a screenshot quoting a message from Amber's ex-boyfriend. It read:

Autopsy report came back, there was a LOT of GHB in Amber's system, only a little bit of coke. Amber was raped. She also had bruises on her back and legs.

Autopsy report won't be released to the public until investigation is done because they know the media will all be doing stories on the case.

Brad added his own comments:

That's fucked up bro.

Hudson killed her ass, what a fucking idiot

That dumb ass been drugging girls for years

This didn't make sense. I don't know much about police procedure, but it seemed weird that the autopsy report would be released five months after Amber's death, and only to her ex-boyfriend. I called Brad. I knew the ex-boyfriend disliked me, so my first thought was that he was just trying to stir the pot. Maybe he was trying to get Brad on his side to entice me to say something stupid.

Our conversation was really odd. Brad kept after me as if he were interrogating me, trying to force me to make a statement on the phone.

"Just say Hudson drugged Amber," he insisted. "Why won't you say it? He for sure killed her, just say it, Eli!"

"I'm not going to say that," I replied. "I was not there when they found her dead, I don't know what happened, and that's the truth. What more do you want me to say?"

Dakota was sitting next to me on the couch. She could hear what he was saying, and she kept nudging me and whispering that I should get off the phone. She sensed it was a trap and thought he might be recording me.

No way. Brad is a good friend. No shot he is trying to set me up. I've known him for years. He just hates Hudson.

Dakota rolled her eyes and looked at me like the fool I was. Meanwhile, Brad kept at it on the phone.

"Dude, just say it! That idiot has been drugging girls for years, I know about it! He killed Amber, just say it."

Hudson wasn't a good friend—he was just another of many nightlife acquaintances I had. I wasn't going to protect him, but I also wasn't going to say something I didn't think was true. I believed from the beginning that Amber died of an accidental overdose, and that hadn't changed with the so-called autopsy report. I wasn't there, I don't know what happened. Sure, I'd seen Hudson party hard. I'd seen Amber party hard. We all partied hard. But I never saw him knowingly drug anyone, and I wasn't going to say I did.

Brad would not let up and would not get off the phone. Finally I said, "Dude, Amber was willingly partying, as I've told you before.

To prove it to you, she texted me saying she took G that morning. I have the text message."

"Bro, why didn't you just say that from the start? That changes everything. Okay, all good then! Send me that screenshot of Amber's text when you can."

Something wasn't right. Dakota's intuition knew it for sure. I was blinded by my friendship with Brad, but my gut told me to be careful. I wasn't going to send him anything.

Keep your distance, Eli. Keep your distance.

NINE

SOLITARY SIRENS

"Nobody can bring you peace but yourself."

—RALPH WALDO EMERSON

THAT STRANGE DECEMBER PHONE CONVERSATION with Brad wasn't the only time he and I had spoken in recent months. In fact, he had been the positive catalyst for a major change I made in my life, beginning in the fall of 2017.

In late summer, I got into new hobbies, including running. I started each day with a three-mile run on the treadmill at Equinox. Eventually I could sustain a six-minute-mile pace. I began recording these runs and posting them on my Instagram story. Brad, who had competed in some intense athletic challenges and liked to push his friends, shot me a message.

"Why don't you try running longer than three miles and slow down your pace?" he asked. "See how long you can run for. You're not even getting your cardiovascular system moving. You have to run longer than twenty minutes to even get it going."

The next morning I doubled my distance to six miles and slowed my pace down to a 7:30 mile. It seemed very easy—I felt super relaxed, like it literally was nothing. I was sure I could run much longer distances.

As you know, I don't do anything half-assed, and I commit hard. I popped onto Twitter and wrote, "Going to run a half-marathon or full marathon in the next few months, it's now on the bucket list."

A friend named Ben Baller, a famous celebrity jeweler, threw down a quick challenge in response. "You ain't running shit! If you can complete at least 70 percent of a full marathon without walking, I'll host Warwick for free and be nice to your best friend for the rest of the year."

I thought that was hilarious, and so did a lot of my friends and people in the industry. The challenge was on, and I was pumped up. No way I could back down now.

I began to train hard every week. I had my eye on the Rose Bowl Half Marathon, which was scheduled in Pasadena for January 21. Running became part of my daily routine, and I found myself feeling like I was falling asleep as I pounded away on the treadmill or in the streets of LA, especially after I passed the five-mile mark. I later realized that I was dropping into a meditative state. I had never felt more free, alive, and happy than when I was running—I truly was experiencing the runner's high, which is a release of natural endorphins caused by extended exercise.

All of this was new to me. At first, I thought someone was spiking my water. *Why do I feel so great?* I had never given much thought to meditation—it was just a bunch of hocus-pocus to me—but here I was, meditating without trying, and the effects were incredibly powerful. I felt amazing. Running was shifting my mindset. It put me on Cloud Nine and showed me how good I could feel without any drugs at all.

I woke up at 4 a.m. on January 21, 2018, to the annoying sound of my iPhone's alarm. I had taken Saturday night off from Warwick—I needed a good night's sleep before my first half-marathon. I woke up nervous and excited, with chills running down my spine and goosebumps flaring across my skin. I was going to race!

Dakota came out to cheer me on that cold morning. She wasn't my only supporter. My father, who has been an active marathoner for years, had never thought he'd see the day when his son followed in those footsteps. "Son," he told me, "this will keep your heart and mind very healthy. I'm very proud of you. Keep it up." The night before the race, he called and said, "Do good at the Rose Bowlsss, son, I know you will. I love you." His extra "s" never got old.

He was the one who advised me to start with a half-marathon. I wanted to start with the Los Angeles Marathon, which was in March, but I took his advice. Still, I trained hard. In fact, training started to push other things out of my life. Instead of doing drugs and drinking to the exclusion of other important things, now I was training to their exclusion. After a lifetime of craving the love and attention of others, I had discovered how much I loved being by myself. I craved my alone time, my zone-out hours on the treadmill or the streets, running through Studio City, Burbank, Hollywood, Santa Monica, West Hollywood, and Brentwood.

I was learning more about myself than I ever had. I was the happiest I had ever been, yet I still was not in synch with Dakota.

I saw this when we took a vacation to Punta Mita, Mexico. It was a paradise, with our own private pool and villa and a view of the ocean, but I knew I was not meeting Dakota's needs. It was great to have Dakota by my side again, but my training routine always came before anything else. I was hyper-focused on running, working out, running, working out, to the exclusion of her and everything else. I craved escaping into myself, escaping away from my work, my industry, my cell phone, all of it.

I was hyper-focused on the daily practices that kept me sane. My addictive personality was now turned toward health, fitness, training, and the inner work I was doing on myself. In my new way, I was still the old Eli.

Can't spell selfish without Eli.

I could see that I was disappointing her, even as I hoped that if I ignored the truth, the problem would go away. Of course it didn't. She didn't say anything to me. She didn't have to.

Still, Dakota was there when I put my earbuds in and joined the crowd of runners on that frigid morning, cueing up *Everlong* by the Foo Fighters, one of my favorite pump-up tunes. I started fast and was in the top ten runners for a while, even though my hands and feet were numb from the cold for the first twenty-five minutes.

My training involved living clean. I had come into 2018 with four to five months of clean eating behind me—no drugs or alcohol, a strict plant-based diet, and a careful focus on what I ate and why. I allowed myself to cheat on Sundays, with pasta, burgers, ice cream and desserts, but even then I stuck with vegan versions of these foods.

I looked at 2018 as a time of new beginnings, new focus, new opportunities, new intentions, and new results.

How you start your day is how you live your day. Set the bar high, Eli.

All of this was great, but there is nothing like race-day experience to teach you something. As I pounded along Pasadena's streets, I discovered the uncomfortable truth that the butterflies I had felt in my stomach had been trying to tell me something.

I should have taken a shit before the race.

Now, I faced the prospect of trying to run 13.1 miles with my ass tightly clenched and my insides roiling. I was beyond uncomfortable—I was in extreme pain. I had heard other runners advising each other to "just shit or piss yourself if you have to, don't lose time off the race—every second counts."

No way. I was not going to be the laughingstock on the local news as the man who shit himself during the Rose Bowl half-marathon. I quite literally gutted it out until I spotted a blue portable toilet at mile nine. I felt like I'd just seen the leprechaun with his pot of gold at the end of the rainbow.

I nearly dove into that blessed little cabin, where I spent all of two minutes taking care of extremely necessary business before I was back on the course. I finished the race in 1:25:24, a 6:32 pace, including my pit stop. I wasn't racing against anyone else, but I figured my thirty-first-place finish was about eleven places slower than it would have been if I had been able to keep running all the way through.

That race marked the official beginning, at least in my head, of a new chapter in my life. I was starting to see that I had a gift for running. I had done very well in the Rose Bowl race with relatively little training. I was now only interested in competing with myself, bettering myself, and exploring this new direction. I got lots of positive feedback from social media. I came to see that a lot of the people who followed me—celebrities and influencers and people involved with the industry—didn't follow hard-core athletes. They were kind of shocked by what I was doing. I was hearing from people who had millions of followers, like my friend Gerald, also known as the rapper G-Eazy, who told me, "Man, there's no way I could do that. I can barely run a mile. Respect, man."

It seemed crazy to them, and I realized I was unique in my industry. Nobody else was running a nightclub, staying out into the wee hours, then getting up to run at the crack of dawn on little or no sleep as they trained for distance-running events.

I saw that what I was doing could be inspiring to the kinds of people I wanted to connect with: big-name celebrities, entrepreneurs, and strivers all over the world. I felt something I had never felt before: a huge spark of light and joy in my heart because I had discovered a way to share my journey with the world in a way that would show others how they, too, could aim high and move their lives in a positive and meaningful direction. I knew I had to keep sharing my life journey, keep sharing the positivity I was experiencing. This felt so right.

Don't get me wrong—I wasn't giving up the nice things I already had. I still made sure I drove the newest Mercedes Benz and wore the latest Rolex watch. I intended to show that I could have it all. That was part of my image. At least, that's what I told myself at the time. Since those first heady days in early 2018, I have changed the way I think about the material possessions that used to motivate me so thoroughly. In the summer of 2020, I shed most of that baggage, getting rid of my high-end watches and cars. I had grown to where I didn't need that sort of thing in my life to make me feel important or worthy.

Here's the thing: that game is a constant chase with no end and no real meaning. No human being with any real self-awareness, purpose, or direction in life cares about what car I drive, what clothes I wear, what club I operate, what watch I am flashing, or what celebrities are photographed with me. They certainly don't care about how much is in my bank account. Material possessions are objects that come and go and will never define you. Yes, nice things are nice things. That's all they are. They hold no real value. When you achieve them, you get a temporary high in the moment, not much different than what you feel when you snort a line or pound a shot. Then you return to the stress and emptiness you felt before, so you seek more of the same, to push that emptiness away for a little while.

Just like booze and drugs.

What matters to people—or should—is how you impact them. Do you touch their hearts and lift up their souls? Do you inspire and motivate them to do and be better in their everyday lives by sharing your personal experiences? Not just your wins, but also your losses and your journey. You have to be raw and real to give positive guidance, to move those who pay attention to you to gain real meaning and substance in their lives. If I could touch someone that way, that feeling would stay with them. I would have a lasting impact. This became my north star, the objective I strove for in my everyday life. I would take it one step at a time.

* * *

Ten days after that first half-marathon in Pasadena, I felt like the king of the world. That, however, was the morning I found myself handcuffed on a curb while police officers swarmed through my home.

Shortly after Amber's death, an LAPD detective named Rusty had texted me for information. I had responded that he needed to go through my lawyer, which is what my lawyer told me to say. I knew I hadn't done anything wrong, but my lawyer didn't want to give police officers the opportunity to twist anything I might say and use it against me. I was a high-profile, big-fish nightclub partner. It wasn't hard to imagine that cops might want to try to take me down. If detectives could generate a story with a head-line that included the words "Nightclub Owner" and "NFL Star" and "Model's Death," why wouldn't they? They lived for those big headlines. You see it happen almost every week.

Just the grimy world we live in.

After the police stopped me, cuffed me on the curb, and began to search my house, they put me in a pickup truck with another police officer. We made small talk until an older white guy with a big smile on his face walked up to the window of the truck where I was sitting, still cuffed.

"Hi, Eli," he said, with a big smile on his face. "Do you know who I am?"

I did. I could tell—I knew he was the sergeant, a guy named Rusty who had contacted me before. "Nice to finally meet you. While my team is searching your home, is there anything we should be aware of?"

"No, sir," I said. "Nothing out of the ordinary."

"You sure, Eli? I'm going to give you the chance to come clean now if there is. You sure there's no cocaine anywhere in your home?"

"No sir, the place is clean as a whistle. In fact, so am I—I haven't been partying these days."

"Okay. Is there any cash lying around? How much?"

"Yeah, maybe about 5,000."

"All right, Eli, I'll take your word for it." He walked away, toward my house.

Maybe these guys thought I was the Pablo Escobar of Los Angeles. Was that what this was about? The radio crackled with Rusty's voice telling my minder to bring me over to my home. He uncuffed me, and Rusty walked me up my own stairs and into my own kitchen. Then he produced the cash.

"Count it, please."

"One thousand, two thousand, three thousand, four thousand, five thousand and...forty-eight dollars."

"Well, you told me it was about 5,000. Looks like you were a little off, so I get to keep the extra forty-eight dollars," he said, chuckling. Of course, he didn't keep it.

What does he really want? Is he hoping to pin something on me so I'll talk? I just want to get this over with.

"Eli, I want that text message," he said. "The text message Amber sent you that morning. What is the password to your phone?"

I froze. *Brad.*

A month earlier, Brad had been hounding me on the phone, and I told him Amber had texted me to say she had been given "G." I knew Brad hated Hudson and wanted to take him down, but I didn't think he hated him so much he'd sacrifice me. Maybe he meant to. Maybe he didn't, and the cops were acting on their own. But here they were, six months after the incident and only a few weeks after my call with Brad.

Dakota was right. She knew it.

I thought very deeply about my response. I didn't want to anger these guys, didn't want to get deeper into a hole. I thought so deeply, I didn't say anything at all.

"All right," Rusty said at last. "If you don't want to give me your password now, we will figure out the code ourselves. I'll be taking your phone for future investigation."

This was one of the worst days of my life. I felt betrayed. In my mind, Brad had placed me in a terrible position. I couldn't imagine handing my phone over to the cops. All I could think was, "this is my moneymaker." My phone lit up constantly all day and all night, bringing me new deals and new contacts. I couldn't imagine losing it, even if I could replace it.

Let's get this over with.

"All right, Rusty, let's make a deal," I said. "I'll give you my password and save you the trouble. I have absolutely nothing to hide. I haven't deleted any text messages, pictures, or anything. You guys go through whatever you need right here in my house, and give me my phone back when you're done. I honestly don't want to go through the hassle of getting a brand-new phone—my entire work life is based on my cell phone."

I sat on my couch while he talked that over with a couple of other detectives.

"All right, Eli, you got yourself a deal."

I opened the phone and handed it over. I knew my language in the text messages from the day Amber died was awful, but I also knew it didn't really mean anything. It was locker-room talk. Truly offensive, repulsive locker-room talk, but for better or worse, that's just how most people I knew in my industry spoke—guys and girls alike are super vulgar in all kinds of situations. I knew that those messages were no longer private and might well become public, and I was okay with that. The language was terrible, but it didn't have anything to do with Amber. I also knew that I had done no harm to Amber, and the messages on my phone would prove that.

Go ahead, boys, dive right in.

A technician who looked like he could have been in Best Buy's

Geek Squad scrolled madly through the device while at my kitchen counter, taking screenshots of pictures and text messages, asking me questions that seemed like they were testing my truthfulness. Rusty sat on a barstool and chatted with me, asking questions about my life and about the case. The third detective leaned against the wall and listened.

At last, they were done. As they got ready to leave, Rusty turned to me.

"Well, that's that," he said. "But why didn't you just meet up with us beforehand, Eli?"

"I was afraid to," I said, adding that I'd never dealt with the law before and had been following my lawyer's advice.

"Your lawyer is correct. You did the right thing in your position," Rusty said, chuckling. "But thanks for cooperating with us today. As far as we're concerned, you're innocent."

As soon as I closed the door behind them, I called Dakota and pretty much fell apart. The whole experience had been traumatic. "I've been interrogated," I told her through my tears. She dropped what she was doing—she was in the middle of a photoshoot—canceled her day and came over.

My instinct is just to be honest in any situation. Should I have done what I did? Should I have cooperated like that, or called my lawyer? More than anything, I wanted whatever was going to happen to be over and done with. If cooperating in the moment was the way to do it, so be it. I later noticed that the search warrant had an error on it. I suppose I could have protested that, but why? I had nothing to hide.

That evening, Rusty sent me a text: "Do you feel better now?"

WTF?

I had no idea what he was up to. Was he playing games with me? Was he being sincere? I didn't care to find out, and so I ignored it for the moment.

I still have PTSD from that day. Even thinking about it triggers anxiety and butterflies in my stomach. I felt violated. For a while, I had trouble even being in my own home. I hadn't done anything wrong, but I felt I had been treated like a criminal. I got over that feeling by reminding myself that I am innocent, and that I have a great life. It could have been a lot worse.

Every life experience is an opportunity to seek a lesson, and learn it. This experience showed me the power of mindset. I could wallow in my sense of persecution, or I could be grateful for having been exonerated. Change your mindset and you change your life. I know, it's not always that easy, but the one thing you can always control is your mind. You have to put in the work, and at low points that can be incredibly difficult. In the end, the choice is yours. You can either find problems in every opportunity, or seek the opportunity in every problem.

I believe that honesty goes a long way in life. I'm pretty much an open book, as the police found out that day. If you're honest, you know where you stand when you look in the mirror, even if people take what you say and twist it to their own toxic ends. I was about to find that out.

TEN

GOING THE DISTANCE

"The more voluntary suffering you build into your life, the less involuntary suffering will affect your life."

—TIM FERRISS

I N THE END, AFTER MORE THAN TWO YEARS, DAKOTA and I simply could not work things out. I was not going to leave the nightclub world, that much was clear. Work was still a priority for me, and despite two major breakups, I still hadn't changed in that regard. Dakota knew it, and she was fed up. I had figured out something else, too. I had grown in my relationship with Dakota, but ironically I grew away from her, not toward her. I understood now that I had to work on myself, by myself. I was going to have to find happiness by looking within, not by looking to someone else to help me be happy. I was going to face and experience my life by myself as I sought my own version of inner peace and acceptance.

I had been clean and sober for eight months when we finally split in March 2018. I still felt awful about the breakup. I'd felt awful like this before, though, because we'd broken up before. The feeling was much too familiar. In my better moments, I was grateful that this was the last time I was going to have to feel so broken up over Dakota.

Slowly, I had learned a lesson. If I broke up with her and went back to partying and hooking up with other girls, I would end up disappointed, because none of those girls could fill the void left by Dakota. Because I had done exactly this behavior in the past, I had seen that the comparison just left me feeling lonelier, missing Dakota more than ever. Then I would beg and plead with her to return.

This time, I did something else. I stopped dating. I was celibate for five months. I took the advice from a member of the Wayans family, who had told me there was beauty in being single. Until then I thought that being with the hottest girl validated me. Now, I began to look inward, to investigate who I am and who I could become.

I focused my energies on my first full-length running race, the Los Angeles Marathon, which was scheduled for March 18. Racing without Dakota to cheer me on felt odd, but I was racing for myself now, not to prove myself to her or to anyone else. For me.

I ran the 26.2 miles in 3:09:11. I had hoped to do better, but that was still a great time—I was in the top 300 finishers in a race that had 20,000 starters. What mattered more was what I was learning about myself. That race cracked open a door of possibility. I had put in the time, clocked the training hours, been consistent and dedicated—and look what I did! So, what else could I do? I had a new perspective on what was possible for me.

At last, I had learned how to improve myself just for myself.

Running forced me to be inside myself, and with myself alone. I couldn't check my phone when I ran. There wasn't anyone else to talk to. I could only look inside, and what I found in that experience was a kind of bliss I had never known. It was quiet, inside my head and out. I had always done things for others—to make them happy, or for their approval. In running, I began to find a state of self-love and happiness for accomplishing something on my own. I had a feeling of personal accomplishment just for me.

Shortly after the race, I traveled to Miami Music Week. By now I was one of the most connected guys in Los Angeles; an event like this one was essentially a job requirement if I was going to stay on top of my game. I spent the weekend as you might expect: hanging out with top EDM DJs, rappers, and models, hopping from club to club and party to party.

I stayed sober the whole time, even when we were out until 10 a.m. I went straight from the party to the gym, getting my runs in every day. I was so proud of myself.

No excuses.

I made it all the way to the last night. Then I cracked like a fat kid on a diet who had been handed a birthday cake.

One of my "friends" threw me a challenge: "Eli, if right now you do a line of coke and a shot, we'll cancel our flights tomorrow, get a yacht, and take all the girls out on it. C'mon, man, you just ran a marathon! How many people can say that? Let's celebrate!"

What kind of "friends" ask you to do something like that when they know you are trying to stay clean and sober? The degenerates I was hanging with—that's what kind.

That was it: *SNIFF! SNIFF!* And pound a shot.

I could say I was talked into it, but that's not true. We all have to take responsibility for our own actions. You can't blame anyone else for where you stand. That's a result of your own choices. I broke a lot more than my eight-month sober streak that morning. I broke a pact I made with myself. Or did I? Did I really break a promise I made to myself, for myself?

No.

Deep down I knew I had made that promise of sobriety for my relationship with Dakota. Not for me. I had cheated myself out of my own greatness. Hidden inside that promise was an escape hatch: now that she was gone, why bother to keep my own promise? There was no one to upset. No one to hurt. And so I joined the party once again.

No one to hurt but me.

That day threw me way back. I stayed up for almost forty hours, going from boats to clubs to hotels to strip clubs, all the way until I had to get on a plane back to Los Angeles. Was it fun in the moment? Hell, yeah. We had a blast, the way I always do when I drink and do drugs. But it was a temporary high, and when I came down, my mind was lost, my body was hurting. And my soul? No idea where that was. I went back into the hollow, empty place I knew so well.

Back on a sick one like you never left.

I didn't go back to sobriety after that. But I did make some rules for myself. First, I would keep running. That was an important part of my life, and I was logging forty to sixty miles per week, always with some do-good, feel-good, chill, deep, upbeat house music in my earbuds—Rufus du Sol, Camelphat, Jan Blomqvist. I never ran without music; it gave me my flow. I wanted to find another marathon to race in—my goal was to compete (against myself) in two full marathons and one half-marathon in my first year of racing. That seemed like a solid goal, even though I felt I could do a lot more.

I was and am proud of my self-discipline. I didn't know anyone else who could be up pounding alcohol and inhaling drugs until 5 or 6 a.m., then on the treadmill or the street by 8 a.m. to get in eight or ten miles. I might have fallen off the wagon in terms of no longer being sober, but I was not going to fall off the training wagon. I was going to maintain my glitz-and-glam reputation by night and my race form by day. In other words, I was behaving like some sort of manic person.

I wanted to become something other than what I was. In August 2018, I had lunch in Malibu with a close friend of mine named Colson, who you might know as Machine Gun Kelly. We took a photo for social media together, and I said to him, "Man, I'm overdoing this. I'm looking forward to the time when people want to follow me on social media for who I am and what I'm doing, rather than for the business I represent or the celebrities and influencers I'm hanging out with."

I had already dated the hottest girls. I already hung out with famous people. None of that was making my life any better. Maybe I needed to tap into myself, to be alone, and figure out what I wanted to do with my life. I didn't know quite what that would look like, but I was feeling my way toward it.

"You keep doing what you're doing," he said. "It's super inspirational. It'll turn into something, and you won't need to be posting these types of things anymore."

I tried hard to limit my partying to once a month, but I gave myself permission to go full throttle at the three weekends that mattered: Art Basel in December, Ultra Music Festival in March, and my birthday and Coachella Music Festival in April. Those were *theeeee* weekends, the ones that really mattered. For them, I put the pedal to the metal for three or five days, getting little or no sleep. My only care in the world then was to *party!*

Booze and drugs, booze and drugs, just enjoy your time with your friends!

Honestly, even when I was doing this, it didn't feel quite right. Partying no longer felt fully a part of who I had become. I didn't feel that I "deserved" to treat myself this way. In reality, it was just another mask.

* * *

On October 21, 2018, I ran my second full marathon, in Ventura. We started in the cool, crisp, foggy Topatopa Mountains in Ojai, running along nature trails in the mountain air. The route was gorgeous, descending through dry ridges to the sunny, sandy beaches of Ventura County.

I entered the race with my eyes on a bigger prize: qualifying for the Boston Marathon. Boston, which takes place each April, is the world's oldest annual marathon and one of the most famous road-running events on the globe. The only way to get in is to complete another race faster than a maximum qualifying time. The cutoff time for my age group had been 3:05:00 the year before, but for the 2020 race, organizers reduced that to 3:00:00. I would have to run a sub-three-hour race, which is no easy thing.

The Ventura Marathon offered a race-tracking app that allowed anyone to track my progress if they had my bib number and my phone number. A couple of friends of mine, one being the YouTube star Logan Paul, had specifically come to the race to cheer me on, and they used the app to see where I was. About fifteen miles into the race, I stopped playing my music because my phone was low on battery and I wanted my friends to continue to be able to follow me.

I never ran without music. This was uncharted territory.

At first, I was stressed out. Athletes have a rule: don't change your routines on race day. How could I run without music?

It turned out to be an amazing experience. I got to really tap into myself, to hear my breathing, to tune into the sounds of nature around me. I could hear my own footsteps, and I was hyping myself up. I had been addicted to having music on my runs—you couldn't pay me to run without beats in my ears. Now I see that was another crutch, another excuse to not be with myself.

The situations in life where you are forced to do things you don't want to do are the ones that give you the greatest opportunities for growth, strengthen your mind, and teach you lessons that stick. Something as simple as running without music for the last eleven miles of the Ventura Marathon opened a new way of thinking for me. The same can happen for you. Whenever you think you need or want something you can't have, get past it. If you are stuck in certain patterns, if you think "my way or the highway," challenge yourself to break those habits. See how doing that can really nourish and strengthen your mental, physical, and spiritual life.

Running that day without music, I set my sights on another racer who had been about twenty seconds ahead of me for most of the race. I slowly caught up and introduced myself to Matt. We learned that we both were trying to qualify for the Boston Marathon. Neither of us had completed a marathon in under three hours, and that day we had to. For the rest of the race we ran side by side, encouraging each other.

Around mile twenty he told me he runs ultramarathons—races longer than standard marathon length. Some ultras cover 50, 100, or even 200-plus miles. I could not fathom running that far.

We pushed each other for the last 6.2 miles. This was only my second full marathon, and I found myself in immense pain. I was still learning what it took to succeed in this game, and quickly realizing that the name of the game was mind over matter. We got it done, coming in hot to finish in 2:58:52, high-fiving across the finish line. It was a huge accomplishment. I placed 34th overall, but that didn't matter to me. I was only in competition with myself. I had a goal, and I wasn't going to stop until I accomplished it.

The brief conversation I had with Matt that day inspired me. As we crossed the finish line, I felt I could keep going. Even though I was in pain, and the back of my right foot was shredded (the skin completely peeled and the whole bleeding mess looking like it had been barbequed), I wanted to keep running down that sunny beach. Matt had planted the seed of an idea that I could do something that seemed impossible: run an ultramarathon.

You never know who you're going to inspire, or when, or how. I'm sure Matt didn't intend to inspire me, but he did. I felt I could push through the wall of pain that so many runners experience during marathons and longer races and just keep going. With pain comes strength of mind, body, and soul. There is no greater reward than putting in the hard work and accomplishing your goals, whatever it takes.

As 2018 came to an end, my path took a definitive turn. For the first time in my adult life, I was happy as a single man. I was still partying, but I wasn't dating anyone, wasn't even thinking about dating. I felt free at last in my mind, without anyone else close affecting my thoughts or emotions. I was solely focused on myself, creating happiness within and on my own. For the first time, I took the time to look deeply into myself and understand who I am. This experience allowed me to let go of some of my past habits, and in particular to finally let go of Dakota. By the end of 2018, I truly knew I had grown when I understood that I could love her at a distance and be happy for her no matter what path she chose. As long as she was happy, I would be happy. That was what mattered.

I finally had figured out that I was the only person who could make me happy. I felt a kind of inner peace that I doubt most people ever feel. They don't take the time to seek it. Instead, they focus on replacing their last partner (or their current one), constantly sizing up one person after another, as if they are playing a board game with no strategy, no end, and no possibility of filling their inner void. This game leaves most people feeling hopeless, desperate, and depressed.

That used to be you, Eli.

I played this game, and suffered for it. I see now that whatever "happiness" I got from that game was just a temporary high. You can't spend your whole life counting on someone or something to bring you joy. You direct the light in your life. You make your own sunshine. Only you.

My inner work and growth showed me something else. Yes, I was still running a nightclub, and yes, I was still partying with top-tier celebrities, rappers, DJs, models, and athletes. But it wasn't very fulfilling. In fact, it wasn't fulfilling at all anymore. Running a nightclub, driving a luxury car, and hanging out with glitzy people to show off a certain lifestyle became increasingly unattractive. I began to believe I was put here on this earth to do something different than that. I was posting about running, and about being plant-based, and getting a lot of positive feedback.

The nightlife lifestyle doesn't benefit anyone around me in any authentic way. It doesn't help the environment. It is hollow. When I was at the height of my nightlife career and told myself I was living my best life, I actually hadn't even begun to live my best life.

My best life is built around my growing desire to motivate and inspire people around me to live a more purposeful life.

I looked at the life I was living and thought, "You're better than this, Eli." I couldn't just drop out. I still felt the need to run a nightclub. Something was going to have to give me a push to make real change.

That wouldn't happen for a little while.

A passage from Tim S. Grover's book *Relentless* caught my attention, and it stayed with me. Now, don't be alarmed—until 2020 I barely read anything longer than a page, and only if it was on a screen. Books were foreign to me. But I saw this in a screenshot, and I retained it as a powerful summation of how mindset and mental power are the keys to everything you want:

> *The fact is, you can't train your body—or excel at anything—before you train your mind. You can't commit to excellence until your mind is ready to take you there. Teach the mind to train the body.*

> *Physical dominance can make you great. Mental dominance is what ultimately makes you unstoppable.*

> *You will never have a more powerful training tool than this: get your mind strong, so your body can follow. The true measure of an individual is determined by what you can't measure—the intangibles. Anyone can measure weight, height, physical strength, speed...but you can't measure commitment, persistence, or the instinctive power of the muscle in your chest, your heart. That's where your true work begins: understanding what you want to achieve and knowing what you're willing to endure to get it.*

L.A. RUNNING

ELEVEN

IT'S LONELY
AT THE TOP

"Travel is the only thing you can buy that makes you richer."

—ANONYMOUS

T WAS THE ARNOLD SCHWARZENEGGER OF PARTIES— like one of the old Playboy Mansion parties, but on steroids.

The location: a four-story, hundred-million-dollar mansion in Bel Air. This place had a bowling alley, a movie theater, a roof-top mega-pool, tennis court, gym—you name it. For the event, we brought in night skydivers, fire breathers, dancers, DJs, and live performances.

We also had about 2,500 girls in lingerie or costumes depending on the theme of the party. Fewer than 500 guys were admitted, yet thousands of people would be stuck outside the heavily guarded gate trying to finesse their way in.

I was pretty much the gatekeeper. If you were a celebrity, influencer, or anyone with relevance in the city and wanted in, you more than likely came through me. Stars like P. Diddy, French Montana, Maluma, Zedd, and The Chainsmokers were just a few who attended these colossal parties.

It was a reflection of how elevated I had become in my game, how trusted I had become in Hollywood that I was in charge of organizing and planning the highlights of this event and a lot more like it.

That's what a lot of 2019 was like for me.

I was better connected, more trusted than I ever had been. My career was firing on all cylinders. Yet I wasn't satisfied. We all become accustomed to what seems normal to us, even if it seems extraordinary to everyone else. And the parties I was arranging, as amazing as they were, felt ordinary to me. I worked in a shadow of constant self-doubt.

Yeah, this party is good, but I could do so much better. I could achieve so much more.

I guess that's what makes The Greats so great—that incessant inner drive to demand more, do more, be more. For me, no matter the personal cost, no matter the effort, I was determined to be more connected. The people around me told me I was the best at what I did, and the kind of work I was doing reflected that—but I couldn't see it. I doubted and underestimated my strengths and abilities.

This mindset kept me on my toes and kept me at the top of the nightlife business. Of course, because I was in nightlife I was also boozing and doing drugs to fight the loneliness and emptiness I still felt sometimes. Yes, I had found something different and rewarding in running, but that was a hobby. Day to day, I still had to put on the mask and go into battle.

Sometimes the club got so popular that people would pay almost anything to get in. I got offers of ten grand, fifteen grand for a table. But if the club was full, it was full—we couldn't take a chance on the fire marshal shutting us down. Once we hit capacity like that, I got to the point where I didn't even care what people were saying to me. That's when I often did a few lines and a few shots and just started ignoring people. I was starting to feel over it all.

Something felt different for me in 2019. Yes, I was fighting my way to the top, and by outside appearances, I had reached it. I fought to stay there. Yet my heart was beginning to look elsewhere. I thought about how I could ease out of the nightlife world, retain all the connections I had worked so hard to build, and put those to use for a greater good and a higher purpose. I didn't know exactly what that was going to be. Looking back, I know I was waiting for some kind of kick in the ass to convince me to step away from this livelihood I had worked so hard to build, and step into something new.

I got that shove after completing the Chicago Marathon. I ran several races in 2019. First I repeated the Rose Bowl Half Marathon in January. Chicago came late in the year, October 13. I ran my fastest time ever, 2:57:15, for an average per-mile pace of 6:46. I am not a professional athlete—I was doing this for fun. I began to wonder, what if I really trained hard and took this seriously?

What if you weren't living in both worlds and instead focused on what you truly love? How far could you take this?

I had ideas—a million ideas—but I still wasn't ready to leave what I had worked so hard to achieve.

Like I said, I was still partying. My birthday blowout in April was the biggest ever. And after the Chicago race, at that night's dinner, I heard a familiar voice.

It's cool bro, you just ran the Chicago Marathon, live a little!

That night turned into a full-on bender. It culminated at 7 a.m. with me body-slamming a 275-pound Russian man named Vladimir into the coffee table in the living room of his very, very nice penthouse. We were both high, and he had slammed me into a wall, saying my dancing gave him a flashback to when he was a kid and other kids picked on him. I wasn't going to take that. (We messed that coffee table up pretty good, but we're still friends!)

No matter what good I was doing myself training as a runner, no matter how great I believed my mental health was, no matter how much I felt at peace with myself, no matter my hobbies or training or daily routines, at the end of the day I was still immersed in the nightclub party lifestyle. It was always there, always available, and I consistently succumbed to the temptation to sneak back in whenever I could make up a good enough excuse for myself.

I wasn't even enjoying my rages anymore. Even in the middle of a blowout, I would get anxious thinking about the consequences: the hangover, the let-down, the impossibility of sleeping for a day or two, the week of putting my life back together. This kind of self-abuse wasn't worth it anymore. It pulled me in the opposite direction of where I wanted to go. I came to see that if I needed booze or drugs to hang out with someone or be at some event, then I shouldn't be hanging out with that person or going to that event.

I was still recovering from the Chicago blowout when my best friend Jesse Waits gave me the kick in the ass I needed (and was ready to receive). Get out of here, he said. Let's get on a plane and see some of the world.

Jesse was one of the most successful nightclub owners I know. He also was one of the most selfless and generous. He knew me well, he knew what I was going through, and he was able to see what I needed. But travel? That had never been on my radar. I'd always been terrified that if I left Los Angeles, even for a little while, I would quickly become irrelevant. Hell, I wasn't able to put my phone down to enjoy an evening or a weekend with Dakota, I was so worried about not keeping up with the latest. How could I possibly remove myself from the mix for weeks?

"Dude, get out there and live," he said. "This is what you worked hard for all these years. Go see the world. December will be your slowest month of the year anyway. Learn to let go a little bit! Let's do this!"

I trusted Jesse. And he wasn't just saying I should get on a plane— he was inviting me to join him, a friend, and a group of models. We would take the party with us! Jesse and I brought along fifteen models, promising me that "we'll be treated like kings wherever we go." We went to London, Milan and Phuket, staying in the sickest hotels, resorts and houses, eating beautiful dinners, partying on insane yachts. I was sick of partying—I had an internal fight with myself every time I had a drink, and beat myself up when I did party—but I appreciated Jesse's generosity and wanted to have a good time with him and for him.

At last, we landed in Bali. And Bali—my experience in Bali was completely different. The whole vacation was fantastic, but Bali touched me profoundly.

Bali was magical, a place that seemed out of a fairy tale. I find it far, far out of the ordinary. Bali is the least-developed place I've ever been; it's not super-clean, but none of that mattered. The people, who had very few material possessions, simply wanted to help me, whatever the situation. They didn't want anything in return—that was just their nature. I had never experienced anything like this culture.

I was sober almost the entire time I was there. I got up at the crack of dawn to work out and explore as much as I could, hiking in the cool mornings between vivid green rice paddies. I wasn't going to waste any time as I explored the waterfalls, beaches, hiking trails, and coral reefs.

Tukad Cepung Waterfall, Bali

After five days, everyone but Jesse and I departed for Los Angeles. We chose to extend our trip, to drink more deeply of Bali and explore more of it. We simply weren't ready to leave. On a whim, I texted Dakota and invited her to join us.

"You will love this place," I wrote. "It has your name written all over it. Just come for five days. Your birthday is coming up—this will be my gift to you."

"Eli, you know this is the craziest idea you've ever had, right?" she replied. "This is nuts! I can't believe I'm agreeing to this. Okay! I'm coming!"

Before we were lovers, Dakota and I were friends. Keeping her as a friend was deeply important to me. Still, I had butterflies at the prospect of her joining me. I wasn't going to get back together with her—I really did find inner peace at last after our final split in 2018. I was genuinely happy on my own. But I will always love Dakota, and it has always felt right to have her as a friend. Her decision to join me was a great gift. She was always going to make me weak at the knees, and a piece of her would always be with me. I was excited to show her the new me—who I was becoming. Her decision to join me felt like a miracle. I chalked it up to the Bali magic.

Jesse had been right. Travel is a mind-bending experience, and it was good for me. I loved the entire trip, but Bali spun my brain. I had never encountered anything like the Balinese culture, which is rooted in the idea of generosity. Indonesians are polite, always smiling, and seem only to want to give, expecting nothing in return. I began to connect to the idea of being less ego-driven, more in service to others after spending time in Bali.

This was a joyous way to live. It was 180 degrees opposite from the world I knew in Los Angeles, where "if you can't be used you are useless."

What an awful mentality.

Los Angeles and the nightclub industry are characterized by powerful self-centeredness. Almost everyone is out for themselves, first and foremost. That way of thinking was so common it seemed normal to me. Only when I got to Bali did I question it and see it for what it is. The Balinese culture of generosity is an example of how all of us should live. The lifestyle is simple, you get around on a Vespa scooter, the vegan food is amazing, and the American dollar goes a long way. I loved all of it.

I ended up staying in Bali for two weeks, and staying away from Los Angeles for a full month. My life didn't fall apart. Instead, it got clearer and better.

This change of setting and change of culture spun my brain, as I said, and I began to think that maybe I could do something here. Maybe there was a future for me in this place. Jesse and I talked a lot about moving here, finding a way to do business in Bali. "Ballin' in Bali," we told each other. I wasn't quite convinced that was right for me—not yet, anyway. I still had more to do in the States.

Camaya Bali

TWELVE

A BLESSING IN DISGUISE

"It is during our darkest moments that we must focus on the light."

—ARISTOTLE

I WANTED A NUDGE FROM THE UNIVERSE. WHAT I GOT was a huge shove from a social change website called Change.org.

It was anything but pleasant.

When I got home to Los Angeles in early January 2020, I went through a bit of culture shock. For the first time, I wasn't excited to be flying into LAX. The city didn't feel welcoming. It didn't feel like home.

Turn me around! Back to the island of Bali, please!

Right away, I fell back into the toxic grind of empty people who live behind the façades of their own masks, working at Warwick, sinking again into what I now saw as the ooze of a fake and fraudulent industry. Every night, I put on my mask and did what I was good at, but my heart wasn't in it. I knew that somehow something was going to give me a sign to move away for good from the debauchery and toxicity. I didn't know what that would be—I just knew I had to go out, play ball, and see how the game that was my life developed.

We started to hear about this thing called "COVID-19," but the nightclub business kept going strong, even as cases began to show up. After all, the party must go on! The last hurrah for me and for many people I knew was another huge blowout at the hundred-million-dollar Bel-Air mansion on Valentine's Day. Brad, of all people, hired me to organize it.

He and I had cleared the air after the police had stopped me and searched my house. We spoke frequently, and I was convinced that I could trust him again. When I told him about the police visiting my house, he seemed genuinely shocked and felt bad. He had spoken to them, he said, but he hadn't directed them to me. Our relationship was important to both of us, and so I chose to accept his version of events and move on.

As usual, we put on an epic bash. Maybe *the* epic bash. It was the mega-party of all mega-parties, with all the girls in lingerie, skydivers flying in at night, A-listers, models—you know the drill by now.

Most likely, that is the last bash like that we will see in this life.

Farewell and good riddance.

Like so much of the country's economy, the nightclub business shut down in March. Warwick, like Hollywood's other clubs, closed, and a year later it still hadn't reopened—who knows if it ever will. A majority of the clubs in Los Angeles are too deep in the hole. Like it or not, I was out of the toxic stew for good—and I liked it. I took this turn of events as my cue to get fully clean and sober, and to promise myself I was going to stay that way.

Until then, the way I behaved had been driven by what other people thought or wanted—or what I believed they did. Now, in early 2020, I knew that there is no better feeling than knowing I wanted the changes I was making for me, and me alone. I had a few more long nights, and each time I woke up and asked, "What's the point?" I knew I was going to get sober, for myself this time, and I began telling people "no," which was new for me.

All the sick, twisted, bender nights were behind me. I would not go there again. For the first time in my life, I was making choices by myself, for myself and myself alone. I decided to better myself, to make the changes I was making, for me. Not for Dakota, not for someone else, not a particular event.

Not this time around, buddy.

COVID-19 changed a lot of things for a lot of people. You might think that was what caused me to rethink and redirect my life, since the nightlife world was now closed. It got me started, but what really pushed me over the edge was a distant echo from the tragedy of Amber's 2017 death.

Back in July 2019, Amber's parents filed a wrongful-death lawsuit against me, Hudson, Noah, Sky, Warwick, and The Highlight Room. Yet I never even heard about it because I was not served papers (when you are sued in civil court for damages, a sheriff's deputy or legal process-server must physically deliver the papers to you, and that never happened to me). I'd never been sued for anything, so all of this was new to me.

I finally found out about this lawsuit in early 2020, when I read about it on social media. I was formally served papers on April 13, the day before my birthday. Since I hadn't been told anything about it, at first I assumed it had gone away, or I had been dropped from the suit. I had no idea I was still named as a defendant. I have since learned that in a civil case (where someone seeks monetary damages, as compared to a criminal case, in which the government prosecutes a crime and can put a defendant in prison), lawyers name as many potential defendants as possible. For them, a lawsuit is like a game of chess. They cherry-picked information from the police investigation to make me look as bad as possible.

I hadn't done anything wrong, so I decided the best thing to do was lay low and let things play out.

Of course, this is Los Angeles, and if there's one thing toxic people like to do here, it's tearing other people down. Alex, the guy who ran TheGrime and had tormented me with lies and falsehoods shortly after Amber's death, got back to work. From my understanding, he had been run out of TheGrime, but he was very active on Instagram and worked hard to get people to follow him. He got up to his twisted, sick ways—and fast. Once again, he started posting provocative statements, taking screenshots of my old texts to make me look guilty. He created "highlight reels" of snippets of the lawsuit to make me look as bad as possible. He left timestamps out of his screenshots of text messages. He made it seem like Amber's last words before she died were her text message to me in which she asked me to come out of my room and check on her. There was no mention of the fact that I actually did that. He left the impression that I was a coward for allegedly ignoring her, and implied that she had died in my home, which she most certainly did not.

A few weeks before he started doing this, Alex had asked me out to lunch to "catch up." I think now he was hoping to get dirt from me or on me.

Because of COVID-19, the whole city, the whole country, was in lockdown. People were bored. It was the perfect environment for trolls, haters, and mindless people who don't look beyond headlines or think for themselves to decide they had all kinds of opinions about me. The majority of people aren't going to go searching around the internet to read the full story or, in my case, the full forty-page lawsuit. They respond to whatever a friend shows them, or whatever clickbait brings them in.

That's exactly what Alex was counting on. If he could stir the pot hard enough, if he could generate enough traffic to his Instagram account, he could direct people from there to a website for more details, where he could profit by selling advertising.

The root of all evil.

The people with the most to say, the people with the strongest opinions, usually don't take any time to actually understand what they are spouting off about. They are just loud-mouthed, close-minded individuals who desperately seek attention. Sadly, the world we live in is dominated by such angry, dark-minded trolls who project their negative energy out into the world and onto any victim they choose, with no accountability. I was attacked by women who asserted I was drugging and raping women, that I was an accomplice to murder. I knew that no such thing had happened, and that when Amber, Hudson, Sky, and Noah left my house that morning, they looked just like thousands of guests I had watched leave nightclubs over the years. The haters just wanted attention, but it was hard on my mental health.

The attacks against me on social media were relentless. I had never been bullied so aggressively, and it took a real toll. I found myself crying a lot, pacing around the house, unsure what to do, believing everything I had worked for was being torn away unfairly. At one point I sat in front of a mirror and stared at myself. In that moment, I understood how famous people feel when they are trashed in public. That was rock bottom.

Not that Alex cared. All he wanted was more reactions, and he especially wanted a reaction out of me. He poked me with any stick he could find to get me to react, doing everything he could to keep the story alive. And people were falling for it—viewership on his Instagram kept growing.

I knew my text messages looked terrible for me, and when they were taken out of context they looked even worse. Plus, the lawsuit included screenshots of a text exchange between Brad and me in which Brad claimed he was a cop. I had told Brad over the phone what had happened, then texted him to say, "Keep what we spoke about between us please." Because it looked like I was saying that to a "cop," selected screenshots of the texts made me look even worse. That's exactly what the lawyers wanted—to make me look as bad as possible. It was working.

All kinds of messages were floating around the internet, including messages I didn't write but which were attributed to me. People dredged up the fake messages Alex or someone else had attributed to me on TheGrime, and it seemed that everyone was dissecting what I wrote, what the lawsuit said, and what I wasn't saying to make me look as bad as possible.

Stories appeared in the media that looked like they had Brad's and Alex's fingerprints all over them. Clearly, my "friend" Brad was still out to get Hudson, and he still wanted me to say that Hudson had drugged and raped Amber—something he was saying publicly—which I was not going to say.

Keep calm. Ignore the noise. This too shall pass.

I really, really did not want to reply. I did not want to be a pawn in Alex's game, and I did not want to draw more attention to his "story" from early April. Ironically, when people posted birthday congratulations for me on April 14, that breathed new life into the controversy, calling out the trolls who tried to shame people who were saying nice things about me. The stress on me was enormous.

Somebody started a petition on the social change site Change.org, to pressure the Warwick partners to cut me loose and pressure the industry to blacklist me from the nightlife world. The petition was full of false and misleading information, alleging that I drugged women, invited friends to rape women, ignored Amber's calls for help, showed no remorse, and colluded with the police to hide evidence. Of course, these charges created more anger and confusion among those who saw the petition. Still, thousands of people signed.

I knew I just had to let it be, that I couldn't respond. My strategy was to give things time and step away from the social media storm until things calmed down.

I was behaving like a crackhead with my phone, neck-deep in the poisonous stew spewing from my screen all day every day. I scanned each and every negative comment and went out of my way to search for hateful messages. I refreshed my social media pages continuously, searching for more and more hate. I really was losing it.

I concluded, "enough is enough." I had to have a voice. I couldn't let "them" speak over and for me, filling the space with false accusations, misleading stories, and fake messages that were spreading like wildfire across social media.

On April 18, my partners at Warwick called and said they wanted to part ways. My first thought was, "What a bunch of cowards. These are the times you guys should be standing beside me and taking my back." They knew the truth. They knew I did nothing wrong. They knew I kept Warwick at the top of its game with blood, sweat, and tears for five years. Had they stood by me, that would have been a bold statement, and the right thing to do in the face of the social media mob. But they were feeling the pressure. "Cancel culture" was on the rise, the #metoo movement had a lot of energy behind it, and they were under a lot of pressure. To pour salt in the wound, they put out a public statement about my leaving the partnership. I asked them to wait until I said something public, but they wouldn't. I knew that would make a bang in the nightlife world and wasn't going to help my case in the public eye.

I wanted the universe to give me a kick in the ass, and it certainly delivered on that. When I thought about it, I didn't really care that much about leaving Warwick. I wanted to get out of the nightlife for a while, and now I was. With a little space and time, I can see that they cut me loose because they were fighting for their business lives. COVID-19 had closed the club, and they didn't know when or if they would ever be able to open again. The controversy around my involvement was a drag on the business they simply couldn't afford. In the end, I wish them nothing but the best.

My addiction to the toxic social media feeds worried Dakota and Jesse a lot. They staged an intervention with me at Jesse's house.

They sat me down and talked me into letting go of everything I used to build my professional success and personal brand: my phone, the phone number I'd had my whole life, all my social media accounts. Everything. They knew my phone was the worst addiction of all my addictions. It had to be broken once and for all.

I knew they were right.

On April 18, I changed my phone number. On April 19, I put this statement on all my social media accounts. Everyone close to me advised me not to say anything, but Warwick forced my hand. I had to. This is what I wrote on my Instagram account:

To my friends, family and anyone I have let down...

In regards to my text messages from 2017, I take full accountability and responsibility for the language and substance of those texts. They were inappropriate, hurtful and disrespectful and there is simply no justification for it. Those messages are not how I view women. I regret every message I had sent that morning. I'm very close with my mother, my sister and various other women who have played very meaningful roles in my life. I want to offer my sincere and heartfelt apologizes for my inexcusable words. Most importantly, I want to apologize to Amber's family about how the substance of my text messages may have affected them during a dark and sad time in their lives. I feel terrible about it all and I have a lot of regret.

There has been a lot of speculation and false assumptions in the circulating social media posts regarding this tragedy. There have also been a number of fake messages regarding Amber's passing that have been falsely attributed to me, both recently and from the past. Please understand that I'm not responsible for these fake posts and I had nothing to do with them. I understand how anyone would be enraged or upset about these posts, just as I am.

The text messages I did write back in 2017 were not leaked. Rather, when the police came to my home after Amber's passing, I willingly provided my password to law enforcement to search my phone and I fully cooperated with them for the sake of being totally transparent. I let them take whatever information they needed from my phone, knowing they could be made public. I fully cooperated to answer every question they had regarding this tragedy.

I want to make it very clear that I did not give any illegal substances to Amber. I did check on her to make sure she was ok after her last text messages to me. After checking that she was okay, I walked her and 3 other people that were at my home that morning to the front door where we all said goodbye. Everyone appeared in good spirits and in good shape. I later learned that Amber and the others went to Amber's friend's house where they continued to party for numerous hours, where I was not present.

Still, this explanation is a separate issue from the regrettable language that I have used in my 2017 text messages. For that, I can offer no justification and no excuse. I can only offer an apology and express my deepest regret. I had been advised against making any statements due to an ongoing civil lawsuit involving a lot of people. However, some things can't go unsaid. I understand that the contents of my text messages are troubling and hurtful. I can't take my words back or unring that bell. I have felt ashamed, embarrassment, regret and disappointment in myself.

During the last 3 years since this tragedy, I've had a lot of time to reflect on my life. From the bottom of my heart, I have the deepest empathy for Amber's family and friends. I continue to be saddened by her loss, and I realize that my sadness pales in comparison to those close to her. I also offer my deepest apologies to everyone that I have caused anger, pain and disappointment to as a result of my language.

Two days later I moved this statement onto my personal web page (www.eliwehbe.com) and disabled my social media accounts. I was being harassed, and my friends were being harassed. A number of women added the fake comments attributed to me to their Instagram stories and trashed me for them, calling me a "scumbag," among other things. Alex was a complete savage. To type something like that and attribute it to me was next-level shittiness. I didn't hear about it from any of my friends because they, at least, could see it for what it was. Once I took my accounts down, I knew that "they" would have no target. It certainly would be the best thing for my mental health.

Brad texted and told me "your apology is stupid as fuck," adding that if I didn't make a statement about Hudson, I deserved the heat I was getting. That was as good as an admission that he was behind all the negativity about me on social media. I shouldn't have been surprised. How many times had I seen "friends" in Hollywood turn on people and beat them down?

Disconnect and reflect.

I cut myself off from the toxic whirlwind just in time. I was in terrible shape emotionally. I've never contemplated suicide, but I understand why people would when they are subjected to unending bullying, taunting, and harassment 24/7. I had never felt this much hate before.

Dakota and Jesse know me well. Their intervention was an enormous gift of love. It saved me. I am beyond grateful to have such amazing friends in such a devastating time. Cutting myself off from social media was one of the greatest choices I have ever made.

Free at last!

Finally free from the soul-sucking addiction to my phone, I was able to focus on what matters in my life. As I write this book almost a year later, I feel so deeply at peace with that decision.

I promised myself that I would not personally look at anything going on in the media. That would just slow me down as I turned toward mapping a new path into the future. I trusted a few friends to keep me informed if anything truly deserving of my attention happened.

Eventually, the hate storm died down. People began to see my perspective, to accept that I had used shitty, disrespectful language but meant no harm to anyone. I even ran into some women I knew who had been bashing me on social media, and they apologized to my face. They admitted they hadn't taken the time to dig into the truth and understand the full story. I appreciated that, but it would have been nice if they also had gone back on those social media platforms and publicly retracted their earlier statements, which they did not do. The damage was done. It was simply something I was going to have to live with.

I lived by my reputation in the nightlife industry, a reputation I spent almost a decade building. I died by it, too, even though I had done nothing wrong besides being vulgar and disrespectful. But I don't hold grudges. Those just make you bitter. Holding a grudge is like jumping into the sea while holding onto a ship's anchor. If you don't let go, you'll drown. Letting go will always set you free.

My decision to put out a public statement and then go dark on social media was one of the best things I could have done.

People like to kick people when they are down. Most don't care and aren't going to help you. I had to inspire and motivate myself— nobody was going to do that hard work for me. The mindset of wanting to be better than who I was yesterday, wanting to do that only for my own growth and not for someone else—that is what flipped my life 180 degrees.

The very worst moments, when you wish everything in your present and your past were different, when you feel stuck in a hole and cannot dig yourself out no matter how hard you try, when you do everything to keep fighting, keep pushing through no matter the price—those are the moments I call *the ones*. *The ones* are the bottom-of-the-barrel moments you wished you never had to experience, but they are where your growth happens. They are why and how you became who you are today. Those miserable situations are what strengthen and mold your mind—at least, they are if you have the right mindset. They are if you are determined to find the opportunity, to turn the negative into the positive.

The greatest leaders are those who have been to hell and back, who have been through crazy bullshit. They hit rock bottom in one way or another, pulled themselves out, and used their mistakes as a guide to better themselves and to create inspiration and stepping-stones for others.

There is a saying in sports, "There is winning and learning." Even if you are defeated on the mat or the field or wherever you might be, you can learn from that defeat. This mentality is what I chose to embrace.

THIRTEEN

INFINITE

"One of the most difficult things is not to change society, but to change yourself."

—NELSON MANDELA

IN MY EARLY TWENTIES, I GOT A TATTOO ON MY CHEST reading "Nunquam Cede," Latin for "Never give up." It meant a lot to me then, and it means more to me now. Nothing in life worth having is going to come easy.

As you have seen, I'm an extremist—there's no moderation with me. I hate moderation, actually. When it comes to something that seems out of the ordinary, even kooky, you can bet I'm figuring out how to get it done. I like to be the oddball, the outcast, the crazy one. I want people to look at me and say, "Damn, he really did that? Respect!"

Anything that makes me uncomfortable is appealing. That's a

good place for me to start. I find something extremely satisfying in putting myself in unbearable, miserable, agonizing physical situations. There's no greater reward than at the end of those roads.

When I commit to something or someone, whether it's building a career in nightlife or loving Dakota or finding out how great a runner I can be, there is no holding back. Whatever you are working for is going to take time, patience, hard work, and consistency to achieve.

When I ran the Ventura marathon, my goal was to break 3:00:00 so I could compete in the Boston Marathon. I achieved that. My next goal was to run a marathon at a pace of 6:30 per mile or better. That was much faster than anything I had accomplished so far.

I expected that to take me many years to achieve. In fact, I thought it would be damn near impossible.

The 2020 running of the Boston race, the 124th annual event, was canceled on account of the pandemic. Boston is normally run in April. Organizers announced that they would sponsor a virtual race in September. At first I thought, who the hell wants to run a virtual marathon? There would be no crowds, no one to cheer me on, no famous Heartbreak Hill. Then I realized I could be part of something historic. Almost certainly, the race would never be staged this way again.

The race could be run anywhere, tracked and verified using an app called Boston Marathon Virtual Experience. I could run it on my treadmill, which I did. I finished in 2:49:00, for a 6:27 per mile pace.

Mission accomplished.

* * *

Certain individuals are meant to come into your life, play a role in shaping you, and then move on in their own journey. Dakota, who stood up for me in the darkest times, has been that. I found love and light through Dakota, and learned more than she will ever know through our time together. As tumultuous as our journey together was, she set me on my own path to inner peace and happiness. Her role in my life is complete. She is on her own way now, having helped grow and elevate me. Not everyone is meant to stay together, but the love I have for her remains. I am grateful to her for blessing my life with her presence and love.

I also am grateful to all the haters. All the "friends" who turned their backs on me when I needed them. All the back-stabbers, the online sheep, the people full of opinions and empty of knowledge yet unafraid to speak. Unafraid, in other words, to talk shit.

Thank you. The more negativity and hate you throw, the more motivated I become. The comments that used to beat me down now fuel my fire. So a huge shout-out to you angry trolls. Thank you from the bottom of my heart. Thank you for giving me the push I needed.

I'm closer than I've ever been with my parents and sister. They have strongly religious views that I don't share, but we've come to accept each other more fully. They even went plant-based in their diet for a while, and now they eat a largely vegetarian diet—which had a big effect on me as well. We're more connected. I make it a priority to visit them regularly, and the fears they felt when I was in the nightlife scene that something would happen to me have vanished. As I got older, I stopped being ashamed of my Lebanese heritage and culture. Now, I'm very proud of it—my only regret is that I wish I'd paid more attention to Arabic when I was growing up, so I could speak it fluently.

I worked in the nightlife industry for fifteen years. By the time I left, at the age of thirty-two, that was almost half of my life. I still have a lot of life to live, and a lot to give—I'm only beginning! But I've learned a few things that I hope you've learned, too.

If you put yourself out in the world, you will be judged. It's unavoidable. People today only hear what they want to hear. They don't care about facts. Most will interpret what they hear into a narrative that fits into what they believe. No matter what, they will always believe their assumptions and ideas are correct, facts be damned.

We have let social media become judge, jury, and executioner. It is an addictive, toxic place. With little or no knowledge, everyone who has an opinion gets to pretend they are an expert and assert their opinions as facts. They will cherry-pick information to support their opinions, ignore facts that go against the way they see things, and continue to trumpet lies and ignorance.

So—the only thing to do is go on and do what you do best.

Life is the way you want to look at it. It's good or bad by your own choosing. And as hard as it may be at times, you can't blame anyone else for where you stand. What you can do is take advantage of the cards you are holding and do something with them. There is always an upside, always an opportunity inside a crisis or a setback. You can play those cards as a stepping-stone, a learning lesson, an experience to grow and evolve.

People are quick to criticize others for what they see as poor choices or a lack of accountability, but slow to look at themselves with the same critical lens. In Hollywood, I saw almost no one who was willing to step back and examine their own toxic issues and the way their own hurts, tragedies, and insecurities were playing out in their behaviors.

I examined my life and myself because I had to. I had to because I realized if I didn't my life was going to spiral out of control. I saved myself from the thing I thought I wanted—living the dream as a nightlife mogul in Hollywood—and that set me on the path to help and inspire others to lead better, more fulfilling lives.

So yes, you will be judged if you are on social media or at all in the public eye. Some people will love you. Some will hate you. Ignore them all. Focus on your mindset. Focus on the choices you make every day, moment to moment. You will face challenges. How you perceive those situations—and how you respond to them—will make all the difference.

If you've read this far, you may think I'm about to preach to you about how you should avoid the path I took into the dark, toxic and fraudulent, star-studded nightlife world.

Far from it.

I wouldn't take back a second of my amazing years at Kress, Playhouse, Warwick, and all the stops in between. I had some amazing nights that will stay with me forever, and I had nights that were terrible. Just as many, probably. Together, they shaped me into who I am. Without going through all that I did, I wouldn't be who I am today. And I love who I am today. I found a lesson in every situation, however wonderful or terrible it was.

That skill is the golden ticket to life. And I feel like Charlie Bucket when he unwrapped the chocolate bar containing Willy Wonka's golden ticket: *I got it!*

Mask off!

BE IN TOUCH

W HEN I GOT BACK ON SOCIAL MEDIA, I DID SO ON December 21, 2020, by posting a four-minute video of me running, filmed by a friend who was biking alongside me. I spoke to the camera, describing my decision to get off social media:

> *"This disconnect was nothing more than amazing, and it changed my life completely. I probably had one of the worst phone addictions ever up until now. I've honestly been the happiest I've been in the last twelve years of my life during this unplug, and I advise any of you trying to take some time off too if you haven't already...*

> *"I'm probably in the best shape of my life mentally, physically, and spiritually...*

> *"I also spoke about the trolls and haters who had bullied me.*

"[You] really do enjoy seeing others go downhill and actually believe that your opinions are indeed factual, with no real knowledge of the situation you're speaking about, which tells me there's some sort of deep dark anger inside of you, and you take that negative energy and reflect it back out onto others, to make yourselves feel better. Which is completely fine, and I wish you the best and hope you find real happiness within your hearts and souls at some point in your life. But to be honest, that hatred put me at rock bottom, deep down in the dirt. I had to grab that shovel and dig myself out one way or another though.

"And in the end, I knew no one was going to help me but me, so I took those cruel and battering comments and used them to push myself to do better and be better. Always know that negative energy will be the fuel to my fire. Maybe you also suffer from drug addiction, acceptance issues, depression, bullying, or harassment. Maybe you also have a dream to be in this limelight of Hollywood, of having some sort of fame or to become filthy rich like I did at one point in my life. Let me tell you, that way of thinking brings zero happiness.

"I hope my story as a nightlife mogul, serial entrepreneur, avid marathon and long-distance runner can inspire and motivate others to see what truly matters in this life. If I can flip my life around, so can you, as long as you work hard for it. I can promise you that much. I'm going to use my platform as a tool to create, motivate, and inspire others by sharing my personal journey and tactics on how I live my everyday life. Always remember this: the weak ones love to thrive on the strong ones' downfalls. But you know what they secretly love even more? A great fucking comeback, and I'm back, baby, better and stronger than ever."

218

I got enormous positive feedback on that post, which in the following few months racked up over 100,000 views and 1,500 comments. Since then I've posted daily about my running and training, how I eat, and so on—just a super-positive message to motivate people.

In early 2021, I ran my first 50K and came in the top ten finishers, even though I did it primarily to learn about running distances longer than a full marathon. In early March, I completed my first fifty-mile race, Mesquite Canyon in Arizona, which is one of the toughest fifty-milers around. I'm working up to some of the toughest ultra-distance races in the country, some of which push 300 miles. I'm going to keep pushing myself until I find my limit.

I love hearing all of your stories, and I want to hear how you are challenging yourself and what inspires you to live a better, more fulfilled life. Find me on Instagram @eliwehbe, or on my website, eliwehbe.com.

Mesquite Canyon 50 Mile ULTRA Marathon

EPILOGUE

As I've shared my evolution toward a healthier, better life, I've heard from a lot of people who want to know what I do each day—my habits and routines. Here are my answers as of early 2021. I'm sure this will change with time, and I urge you to use my routines as suggestions only (after all, I'm not a doctor!). Figure out what works for you, just as I figured out what works for me.

WHAT DO YOU EAT?

I've been eating a plant-based diet since 2017. I experience so many benefits: mentally, physically, spiritually. It's better for the environment, too. There are many good documentaries you can watch to teach you about those benefits. I recommend *The Game Changers*, about one man's quest to learn the truth about meat, protein, and strength. I also like *What the Health?*, *Cowspiracy*, and *Seaspiracy*.

I found a vegan diet really improved my strength and stamina as a runner, and I learned I operate best when I'm almost exclusively eating organic fruit. Since I went vegan, I haven't been sick—only the occasional brief cough or stuffy nose, never lasting longer than two days.

I take the following supplements:

Oil of oregano

Black seed oil

Echinacea Goldenseal

Vitamin C

Turmeric

Vegan B-12

WHAT'S IN THOSE SHAKES & SALADS YOU LOVE?

Here's my go-to shake following a run:

Frozen açai or dragon fruit smoothie packs

Handful of strawberries

Handful of blueberries

Scoop of Nuttzo

4 Medjool dates

Handful of chia seeds

Handful of hemp seeds

1-2 scoops KOS or NUTRALEAF plant-based protein

Flax milk (I like Malibu Mylk)

Hemp or oat milk

Optional: cashew, peanut or almond butter; banana

Throw it all in a blender and have at it!

I love a big salad. You can put all kinds of things in salads, of course. My salads usually consist of:

Organic mixed greens
Lupin beans
Lentils
Pinto beans
Black beans
Olives
Tomatoes
Cucumbers
Quinoa
Avocado
Mixed nuts
Avocado-cilantro dressing (I like Organic Girl brand)

WHAT'S YOUR SLEEP ROUTINE?

I get six to eight hours of sleep a night, and I make sure to wake up early. I've found this is beneficial to all aspects of my life, and believe me, I have been on every sleep schedule in the world. My hectic lifestyle in the past caused me to try all kinds of things. This is the solution that hits the button for me.

WHAT'S YOUR MORNING ROUTINE?

I wake up early. There is no better feeling than being up early, feeling like you're one step ahead of the world, and being productive.

I always make my bed. It's a simple task that can start your day off right. I like to do it because I have OCD tendencies and value order in my life. It runs in my blood to keep my living space clean and tight. More important, doing this little task can affect the mood and direction of your day. It's incredibly powerful. I'm not asking you, I'm telling you: Make your damn bed!

The first thing I do, without fail, is meditate for about twenty minutes. I'm the first to admit that meditating well is not simple. It's a daily battle to be present, to let go of stress and anxiety and just "be here now." My task is always to let go of whatever I'm currently facing or dealing with, whatever is bothering me.

I wasn't into meditation until I hit rock bottom. I needed something to set my mind free. Setting a daily intention during meditation sets the tone for the rest of my day and helps me make a conscious decision about where to focus my energy. I set my intention to always be present, and each and every day I am blessed to be here in this life. I tell myself, "I AM present, I AM leading by example, I AM bettering myself each day and inspiring those around me." I repeat these intentions during my meditation. Those "I AMs" are very powerful. They really make a difference for me. Find what is powerful for you.

If you need help learning how to mediate, I recommend an app called Headspace. It offers a variety of guided meditations, it's very simple, and it focuses on mindfulness. It worked wonders for me, and I expect it will for you, too.

WHAT'S YOUR WORKOUT ROUTINE?

I actually do two workouts daily. One is a run; one is core work.

OKAY, WHAT'S YOUR FIRST WORKOUT?

Before I start any kind of distance run, I foam roll all the major muscles in my body. This has helped me prevent injury. I hit each muscle for about thirty seconds, going all around my body. (You can find lots of videos on YouTube about how to foam roll.) As I write this book, I'm running about a hundred miles a week, so this kind of self-care is critical.

I log all my miles with pen and paper in a journal. It feels better to me to do it that way than on an app or a spreadsheet. It is more meaningful and makes me more accountable to my goals. After all, you're only cheating yourself if you don't hit your goals.

Every single time I step on the treadmill, street or trail, I say, "Man, I definitely don't feel like running today." But completing my runs is the most satisfying reward I know. Running allows me to be completely present in the moment. It is its own kind of meditation. Running is about finding my inner peace, and it changed every single aspect of my life for the better.

Everyone has their thing—running is my thing. I feel at peace and free on runs. It is my creative time, my thinking time, my time to disconnect from the world and learn more about myself. I even talk to myself on my runs, repeating my "I AMs." I coach myself, too, saying things like, "This ain't shit, Eli, let's go! It's light work, easy work! Let's get it done! No one is going to run these miles for you, but you."

When the pain starts to kick in, when I feel like I have no juice left and I am ready to collapse, that's when the shadow work comes in—real mental work. "Dig deep," I tell myself. "You earned this pain. Keep running and enjoy it. Never give up."

You have to keep pushing no matter what. This is true throughout life. You are your worst enemy and critic. Only you can shut you down. Remember, what you tell yourself is your reality. If you tell yourself you are tired, you are going to quit and feel tired. Change that mindset. Tell yourself you have all the energy in the world and you are going to keep pushing no matter what.

David Goggins, an ultramarathoner, former Navy SEAL, and general badass who wrote the book *Can't Hurt Me*, has what he calls his "40 percent rule": "When your mind is telling you you're done, you're really only 40 percent done."

You still have 60 percent left—tap into it!

No one else taught me how to run—I fell into it. Running feeds my extreme personality and my need for endorphins, but I'm getting them myself, rather than through drugs or booze. My runner's high is a next-level experience, and I crave it. This is the best kind of drug addiction. It keeps me healthy, too—I'm lean and in the best shape of my life.

I don't follow anyone else's plan or program, and I don't train against anyone else. I go with what works for me, with the aim of feeling light and loose. I use a lot of trial and error. I am often sore or achy, and I've had some injuries, but nothing beautiful is easy.

As the saying goes, "The journey is the destination." I continue to be open-minded about how to learn and grow in running (and in life), and that's the most beautiful part of all of it.

There is no finish line.

WHAT'S YOUR SECOND WORKOUT?

Keeping my core strong only elevates my running performance. The lighter and tighter I become, the more at ease and relaxed I feel on long runs.

My second workout of the day consists of all core exercises and lasts for approximately one hour without breaks:

Pull-Ups(burnouts)
Push-Ups (burnouts and dumbbell rows)
Planks (burnouts)
Cable machine (twists and crunches)
Seated medicine ball twists and crunches

There are many core workouts available—have a look at YouTube for ideas. These workouts never get easier! The whole point is to challenge your body and mind to achieve new heights.

HOW DO YOU ELEVATE YOUR MIND?

After my run, I cool down and pick up a book. This is a new habit for me. Until 2020, I never read books. In the past I couldn't concentrate on a book, I lost track of what I read, got frustrated, and gave up. I was too worried about the past or the future. Now that I am better at being in the present, I love reading.

Books strengthen the mind. Reading has been a huge asset in so many ways, including motivating me to be better today than I was yesterday. I've been particularly inspired by autobiographies and memoirs. If you want to develop a reading habit, that's where I recommend you start. Find a story that seems interesting or relatable, that makes you smile or your eyes light up. A couple of my favorites are *Can't Hurt Me* by David Goggins, *Eat & Run* by Scott Jurek, *Open* by Andre Agassi, and *Greenlights* by Matthew McConaughey. If their stories don't inspire you, I'm not sure what will.

DO YOU HAVE A CREATIVE OUTLET?

Writing has become extraordinarily special for me—therapeutic, in a sense. I didn't think I would have been able to write a book, but here we are!

Writing was part of my daily routine—I rarely missed a day during those four months. As I engaged this process, I was amazed how much I could remember. If you have a story to tell, sit down and get going. You never know who you could help, inspire, or motivate. There is no better feeling than knowing you changed another human being's life for the better through your own experiences.

You can train your mind to do anything you want. I sat down and started writing, and in four months I had a first draft. Writing this book changed my life, and I hope it inspired you to change yours, too.

NO FINISH LINE

ACKNOWLEDGMENTS

There are a ton of people I could thank, but I'm going to name the very few who rode with me during this rough time in my life.

When I was at rock bottom, depressed, lost, and had no idea what direction or approach to take when false allegations and misleading stories were spreading about me, my friend Jackie Roberts reached out. Whatever it is that you are going to be doing now, she said, this is the best time to write a book, especially on your life. From the bottom of my heart, thank you, Jackie. People asked me to write a book for years, but if not for that conversation in my living room when I truly believed it was the end of the world for me, I wouldn't have written this. Love you.

To my best friend, Jesse Waits, for sticking by my side through thick and thin, for always guiding me to a brighter future and always having my best interests in mind. You fought for me like

I was your own blood. Thank you for always making me see what truly mattered in life and what didn't. Love you, man.

To a great friend of mine, Josh Puente, thank you for picking me up on those extremely early mornings and supporting me on my marathons. For all the days you spent hours with me on the phone letting me vent to you and genuinely caring and listening to everything I had to say. For picking me back up when I felt I couldn't go on anymore. For the days I didn't want to do anything but sit around and be down on myself, making me get up and work harder than ever. You've done so much for me over the past few years. I can't thank you enough. It means the world to me. Much love my brother.

To my running warriors and colleagues Blake Raymond and Matthew Glynn. You both believed in me anytime I wanted to throw in the towel. We've run countless miles together, and I'm grateful to have met you on my running journey. Thank you both for being great friends and inspiring me to keep pushing beyond my limits. See you back on the road and trails, boys.

To Dr. Jason Khadavi. Thank you for being an amazing and supportive friend. I've gone to countless doctors, and you have hit the nail on the head with the best advice. You've done your best to get me in tip-top shape anytime I am injured. You've always steered me in the right direction. You are great at what you do and the best podiatrist around. Thank you for always getting my recovery time down quicker than ever and answering me immediately anytime I need advice. You're the man! Love always, my friend.

I want to thank my mom, Laurie; my dad, Tony; and my sister, Diana. You have shown me what it's like to have a real family, sticking by my side at all times—during my highs and lows and my darkest times. I love you guys. Thank you so much for all that you do.

Finally, I want to thank each and every one of you who have found a jolt of light in my journey, an inspiration to create a more positive path of your own. I felt stuck at one point in my life, and I know you can get out of whatever hole you've fallen into, no matter how deep it has become. You have the power within you to climb out. There is a new path waiting for you. I can assure you that everything will work out the way it is supposed to as long as you work hard towards it. I'm here with you and trust that you, too, will find the light in your life along your new journey.

Made in the USA
Las Vegas, NV
24 October 2023

79670939R00134